GW00802489

# Poetry Ireland REVIEW 78

*Eagarthóir/Editor*

PETER SIRR

Poetry Ireland Ltd/Éigse Éireann Teo gratefully acknowledges the assistance of
The Arts Council/An Chomhairle Ealaíon, and the Arts Council of Northern Ireland.

Poetry Ireland invites individuals, cultural groups and commercial organisations to
become Patrons. Patrons are entitled to reclaim tax at their highest rate for donations of
between €128 and €12,700. For more details please contact:

The Director
120 St Stephens Green
Dublin 2
Ireland

or telephone 01 4789974; email management@poetryireland.ie

*Poetry Ireland Review* is published quarterly by Poetry Ireland Ltd. The Editor enjoys
complete autonomy in the choice of material published. The contents of this publication
should not be taken to reflect either the views or the policy of the publishers.

ISBN: 1-902121-16-3
ISSN: 0332-2998

ASSISTANT EDITOR: Paul Lenehan
DESIGN: Alastair Keady (www.hexhibit.com)

Printed in Ireland by **ColourBooks Ltd** Baldoyle Industrial Estate Dublin 13

# Contents

Poetry Ireland REVIEW 78

## Nuala Ní Dhomhnaill

TÚS AGUS DEIREADH GACH SCÉIL
*i gcead don mBab Feirtéar*

Nuair a tháinig an rábaire scafánta dea-chraicinn
faoi mo dhéin ar deireadh, i gcaisleán mo mháthar,
tar éis dó gabháil trí thine agus trí uisce
lá i ndiaidh lae
faid is a bhí an ghrian ag dul
ar scáth na copóige agus an chopóg ag teitheadh uaithi,
ó mealladh é an chéad lá ag an loinnir sholais
a bhí ag teacht ón dtáth úd dem' chuid gruaige
a chonaic sé ar líne barrataoide go moch ar maidin
agus é amuigh ag marcaíocht na duimhche
ar a bhromaichín giobalach,
bhí san go maith agus ní raibh go holc.

Cé nach mór an fháilte a chuir an tseanchailleach,
mo mháthair, roimis, ach a mhalairt glan,
an doicheall,
is nár thug sí le n-itheadh do
ach canta d'arán cruaidh mine coirce,
próca suibhe a bhí glas le snas
is muga de mhaothal chómh stálaithe sin
go bhféadfá é ghearradh ina dhá leath le scian,

mar sin féin níor ith sé is níor bhlais sé iad
agus níor dhein gearán ar bith
faoin droch-chóir a cuireadh air
ach chuaigh a chodladh dó féin
ar shean-raca de leaba
go raibh spoir iarainn aníos tríd,
rud a dh'fhág go raibh an fear bocht
tinn go maith ar maidin.

Nuair a chuir sí i bhfiachaibh air
dul amach 'on stábla
agus an tsnáthad a chaill a máthair
céad bliain roime sin a dh'fháil di
is go mbíodh dhá scaob déag den aoileach
ag teacht isteach
in aghaidh gach scaob a chuir sé amach,
is mise a fuair an tsnáthad dó.

Bhí rudaí eile leis gur bhodráil sé
mo cheann leo,
ar nós snámh go tóin poill sa loch
i ndiadh fáinne a bhí caillte ag máthair mo mháthar
céad bliain roimhe sin.
Bhíos chomh scaimhte sin chuige gur chuas chomh fada le
trí dheor fola óm' chroí
a scaoileadh anuas sa dearnan aige
chun go bhféadfadh sé iad a chur isteach
leis an gcrann agus an claíomh a bhí ann
a tharrac amach chuige féin.

Bhí rudaí eile, leis, a dheineas dó,
nach fiú liom a insint anseo,
ach thar aon cheann eile acu gur mise
a thug comhairle a leasa do i gcoinne na seanchaillí;
ará is a chur in úil di le fuaimint agus a cur i luí gcaidhte uirthi
má bhí sé sa mhargadh an tsnáthad is an fháinne is an claíomh
a thabhairt chuichi
nach raibh sé riamh i gceist nó curtha sa bhfís aici
iad a thabhairt di.
(Bhain sin cuid den gcaincín di, má dhein aon ní riamh,
táim á rá libh).

Ina dhiaidh sin is uile
nuair a tháinig sé chomh fada lena thí féin
i ndeargainneoin gach comhairle a fuair sé uaim,
cé nár thug sé póg dá mháthair
nó nár rug barróg ar a athair,
cad déarfa leis an liútáil is an únfairt
a bhí ag an gadhairín beag madra timpeall air
ná gur thug sé póg dó.
Ansan ar an spota d'imigh glan as a chuimhne
gach a raibh déanta agamsa dó.

Níl ach aon chloch amháin suas im' mhuinchile agam
nó b'fhéidir nárbh fhearr rud a thabhairt air ná cárta,
agus is é sin cleas an choiligh agus na circe.
Cuirfidh mé síos ar an mbord iad
os comhair comhthaláin na bainnise
is neosfaidh siad an scéal ar fad i gceart
i bhfoirm cluiche.

Ach tá dochma orm roimis.
Cad is fiú dom, ar deireadh
bheith suas agus anuas lem' dhuine?
Nach leor liom mar dhearmhad a dheineas
teitheadh leis an chéad lá ón Domhan Toir,
gan a bheith ag cur anois leis an mí-ádh?
Cuimhním gur fearr go mór a bheinn
fanta go sásta i gcaisléan mo mháthar
dá bur seanchailleach féin í.

Slí amháin nó slí eile
ní bhíonn aon an-dhea-chríoch ar an gcailín
ins na seanscéalta seo.
Fiú nuair a phógann sí prionsa na póige
cad a bhíonn dá bharr aici age deireadh
ach clann is liútar éatar is tuirnín lín
ag rothlú timpeall i gcónaí
de shíor síor agus riamh is choíche
agus cad chuige?

## Gregory O'Donoghue

LAKESIDE

Creek Feather,
sit again on the toes

of the hawk-beaver tree,
tell me midnight stories:

how lunar touches
make beauties of hags,

gleaming dice
of warriors' bones;

or say again the saga
of your Greyhound travels,

San Joaquin
to Wounded Knee,

how you watched
the morning:

wispy clouds –
paint-starved brushstrokes;

or say nothing as night
pauses between

the leaves, the lake
and the whippoorwill.

**Peter Carpenter**

ACHILL

Sweeneys has a line in gravel
and sand, everything pretty much:

breezeblock essentials, vanloads
of speeding undesirables, a fire

of tyres, judging from that billowing
across the water and the bind

of sound from fellas texting
and missing calls. Then there's

the bar that never shuts, flying really
flying… And the front room lined

with candles, a solid swirl
of stairhead, the couple going down

to the beach heightened in buzz
by the 'Govan sheen'.
                                    The lilies

were already there, pouting along
by the path – we just cut them from

wild and found the vases. Around us
no muttering of prayer, just

black-headed sheep tearing away
uncannily into the backdrop

of grey-slicked stone, skylarks
and water, bog cotton. Well after

the last taxi, still the flapping of
peat in plastic bags, miles off.

**Peter Carpenter**

PUBLIC WRITTEN DECLARATION

to set humour at humour's throat

to free art from the dead weight of the real world

to explore flux

to be a machine

to reconcile vertical-horizontal, male-female, heaven-earth

to have it all my own way as often as is humanly possible

to tell stories (I got sick and tired of the Purity!)

to make an intelligible area of the whole wall

to celebrate the blossoming of a new culture and a new civilisation

to get out a little more

to buy that Marlborough *Cloudy Bay* bin-end from Oddbins on my
    way home

to celebrate the strangling of the vulture


to celebrate

**Peter Carpenter**

IN HEAVEN

There'll be a really decent frying pan,
a store of light like it is here just past
nine thirty some immovable June evening,
and a frozen Rapidice jacket thing
to chill another Sauvignon, fast.

**Paddy Bushe**

THE POET PINES IN EXILE IN SUZHOU

The neon sky is sodden with mist tonight,
Discoloured as the canals that carry
Plastic bags under stepped stone bridges
In ornamental gardens. Here scribes and poets
Wrote elegantly of absent friends and distant wives.

Leaves that should compose their own calligraphy
Of loneliness under a clarifying moon
Are limp in its absence. Even poor Li Bai
Had his own shadow to keep him company
And with him raise a wine-cup to the moon.

My shadow lies within myself. And so
I spin a globe and from that shadow
I create a moon. I imagine its clear
Fullness over Binn Mhór, the touch of frost
That makes you settle deeper in our bed.

## Paddy Bushe

FUAIMRIAN

Tá sé ag rith is ag ath-rith
Trím aigne: blúire de scannán
Dubh agus bán creathánach
Ar chlár tromchúiseach teilifíse.

Na caogaidí. An tSín. Mao.
An Léim Mhór Chun Tosaigh.
Cruach á bruithniú go craosach
As seanúirlisí i sráidbhailte
Ó cheann ceann na tíre,
Agus an ghráin dhearg ag an bPáirtí
Ar éanacha beaga ceoil
As gach aon ghráinne cruithneachtan
A ghoideann siad idir portanna.

Sluaite á mbailiú, mar sin,
Ag gach aon chúine sráide
Agus bualadh ollmhór oifigiúil bos,
Á spreagadh gan stad le gártha cáinte
Ag cur na ceoltóirí beaga de gheit
Ag eitilt timpeall agus timpeall arís
Go dtí go dtiteann, ar deireadh, éan
Ar éan de phlimp in ndiaidh a chéile,
Traochta chun báis ar an dtalamh

Níl aon fhuaimrian ceoil
Leis an scannán. Ach samhlaím
Na mílte fliútanna aeracha bambú
Ag boilgearnach leo scathaimhín,
Agus, poll ar pholl, nóta ar nóta,
Samhlaím gob ollmhór dubh á sárú
Chun ciúnais, ceann ar cheann.

Agus samhlaím ina n-áit
Trúmpa mór amháin práis
Ag búireadh an nóta chéanna
Lá i ndiaidh lae i ndiaidh lae.

Sarah Maguire

FROM DUBLIN TO RAMALLAH
*for Ghassan Zaqtan*

Because they would not let you ford the river Jordan
and travel here to Dublin, I stop this postcard in its tracks –
before it reaches your sealed-up letterbox, before yet another
    checkpoint,
before the next interrogation even begins.

And instead of a postcard, I post you a poem of water.
Subterranean subterfuge,
an indolent element that slides across borders,
as boundaries are eroded by the fluency of tongues.

I send you a watery bulletin from the underwater backroom
of Bewley's Oriental Café,
my hands splintered by stainedglass light as I write,
near windows thickened with rain.

I ship you the smoked astringency of Formosa Lapsang Souchong
and a bun with a tunnel of sweet almond paste
set out on a chipped pink marble-topped table,
from the berth of a high-backed red-plush settle.

I greet you from the ranks of the solitary souls of Dublin,
fetched up over dinner with the paper for company.
Closer to home and to exile,
the waters will rise from their source.

I give you the Liffey in spate.
Drenched, relentless, the soaked November clouds
settle a torrent of raindrops
to fatten the flood.

Puddles pool into lakes, drains burst their sides,
and each granite pavement's slick rivulet has the purpose of gravity.
Wet, we are soaking in order to float.
Dogs in the rain: the cream double-decker buses steam up and stink

of wet coats and wet shopping,
a steep river of buses plying the Liffey;
the big circumnavigations swing in from the suburbs, turn,
cluster in the centre, back off once more.

Closer to home and to exile:
I seek for this greeting the modesty of rainwater,
the wet from ordinary clouds
that darkens the soil, swells reservoirs, curls back

the leaves of open books on a damp day into rows of tsunami,
and, once in a while, calls for a song.
I ask for a liquid dissolution:
let borders dissolve, let words dissolve,

let English absorb the fluency of Arabic, with ease,
let us speak in wet tongues.
Look, the Liffey is full of itself. So I post it
to Ramallah, to meet up with the Jordan,

as the Irish Sea swells into the Mediterranean,
letting the Liffey
dive down beneath bedrock
swelling the limestone aquifer from Hebron to Jenin,

plumping each cool porous cell with good Irish rain.
If you answer the phone, the sea at Killiney
will sound throughout Palestine.
If you put your head out the window (avoiding the snipers, please)

a cloud will rain rain from the Liffey
and drench all Ramallah, drowning the curfew.
Sweet water will spring from your taps for *chai bi nana*
and not be cut off.

Ghassan, please blow up that yellow inflatable dinghy stored in your
    roof,
dust off your compass,
bring all our friends,
and swim through the borders from Ramallah to Dublin.

## Günter Grass

ZUM PAAR GEFÜGT

Zwei Buchen einer Wurzel
sacht bewegt, sobald ich
um ihren Tanz den Kreis beschreibe.

Die Stämme glatt und nah bei nah,
daß grad ein Luftzug
die Haut noch streichelt.

Erst im Geäst sind sie behende,
nackt winterlich verzweigt
vor leergeräumtem Himmel.

So bleiben sie im Takt,
verzückt in leichter Beuge.
Weiß nicht, welche ist sie, welche er.

Zwei Buchen tanzen auf der Stelle.

COUPLED

Two beech trees, from a single root,
gently rustle as I
circle round their dance.

Their trunks so smooth and cheek by jowl
that a breeze alone
might stroke their skin.

Only their limbs are supple,
wintry boughs bare
against a cleared-out sky.

Thus they keep the rhythm,
enraptured, slightly arched.
Don't know which is she, which he.

Two beech trees dancing on the spot.

ZUGABE

Nach langem Beifall – Handwerk knallhart –
greifen müde ergraut die Musikanten noch einmal
nach Holz und Blech.

Paare, wie sie gefügt und zufällig beieinander,
bewegen sich zwangsläufig, bleiben,
solange das dauert, im Takt.

Schon räumen die Kellner ab. Wir ahnen, daß demnächst,
wenn nicht sogleich, Schluß ist, hoffen aber
auf Zugaben bis zuletzt.

So verzögert sich allgemein und speziell
unser Ende, das seit langem rot vordatiert
im Kalender steht.

Wer das Licht ausknipst endlich, bleibt im Dunkeln,
hüstelt ein wenig und lacht sich ins Fäustchen.
Kehraus heißt die Polka.

ENCORE

After long applause – tough handiwork –
the musicians, grey and weary, reach once more
for wood and brass.

Couples, paired off at random or by choice,
move around as though compelled, keeping
time for as long as it goes.

Already the waiters clear the tables. We know that soon,
if not quite yet, the evening's up but hope
for encores to the last.

So our end, in general and in particular,
though in the calendar long marked in red,
has been postponed once more.

The one who switches off the lights remains in the dark,
coughs a little and laughs up his sleeve.
A polka's our final dance.


LÄSTERLICH

Heute nacht, Liebste,
träumte mir,
ich läge dir bei.
Aber das warst nicht du,
auch du nicht,
verjährte Geliebte –
nein, natürlich nicht meine Mutter! –,
vielmehr war ich der besagte Erzengel,
und die Jungfrau – jadoch, Maria! –
erkannte mich: beinebreit.

Wollte erwacht lästerlich
meine katholische Herkunft verfluchen,
dann aber begann ich mir Sorgen zu machen
um mein Söhnchen,
des kleinen Erlösers bekannte Zukunft.

BLASPHEMOUS

Last night, beloved,
I dreamt
I lay with you.
But it wasn't you,
and not you, either,
lapsed lover –
and no, not my Mother, of course not! –
rather, I was the Archangel himself
and the Virgin – Mary, yes, that's right! –
knew me: legs spread wide.

When I woke, I wanted to blaspheme
against my Catholic upbringing
but then began to worry
for my infant son,
the little Saviour's well-known fate.

## AUGENBLICKLICHES GLÜCK

Wenn ich beim Kopfstand die Familie zähle
und weiß, daß kein Haupt fehlt,
denn alle bibbern ängstlich und geniert
im Halbkreis stumm,
weil Vater zeigt, was ihm als Greis
so grade noch gelingt –
mit siebzig, fünfundsiebzig
die Kiste hoch, die Beine krumm –,
und ich aus Bodennähe seh,
wie alle Enkel
sind wohlgeraten,
die Söhne, Töchter schön
in ihren Krisen und kopfoben alle,
scheint mir die Welt im Lot zu sein,
auch staunenswert,
solang ich mich kopfunten halte;
dann aber wankt, was nur Behauptung war
und – auf des Augenblickes Dauer –
mich glücklich machte aus verkehrtem Stand.

## MOMENTARY HAPPINESS

When, doing a headstand, I count my loved ones
and know that no one's missing,
for they all sit silently around me,
embarrassed, fearful, trembling,
as Father shows that there's life
in the old man yet (just about) –
at seventy, seventy-five
arse up and bandy legs –
and when from near the floor I see
how fine
my children's children are,
the sons, the daughters beautiful
in their crises and all of them chin up,
the world appears to be quite plumb,
miraculous even,
so long as I keep my head down;
but then I start to falter, as does my headstrong claim
which – for a lingering moment –
had me happy upside down.

KURZ VOR OSTERN

Sah einen Schwan
auf schwarzem Tümpel.
Nicht er, ich erschrak.
Zuviel Schönheit mit Gleichmut gepaart.
Hielt das nicht aus, ging.

Auf dem Rückweg zwei Kröten
unter- wie übereinander,
kaum vom Atem belebt.
So Jahr für Jahr
wie nach Vorschrift.

Ach, stünde die Welt doch Kopf!
Vielleicht fiele ihr was
aus der Tasche.
Der Schlüssel, zum Beispiel,
passend für einen Ausweg.


SHORTLY BEFORE EASTER

Saw a swan
on a black pond.
I flinched, not him.
Too much beauty coupled with composure.
Couldn't bear it, left.

On the way home two toads,
one on top of the other,
hardly animate with breath.
Thus year after year
as though by the book.

Ah, if only the world stood on its head!
Something might fall
out of its pocket.
The key, for instance,
to a door that leads out.

KARA

Unser Hündchen ist tot.
Niemand hebt mehr den Kopf,
wenn ich, weil schlaflos,
nachts die Küche heimsuche.
Im Wald ist mir niemand
drei Schritte voraus
und zeigt an,
wo es lohnt, haltzumachen,
die einzelne Eiche, engstehende Buchen
mit Stift auf Papier wahrzunehmen:
Stämme, Geäst.

Schneller als mein voreiliger Gedanke,
folgsamer, als ich je sein konnte,
treuer, als selbst die Liebe es fordert,
war unser Hündchen.
Wenn ich den Stock weit
in die schlappen Wellen warf,
war ihm nie – mir schon –
die Ostsee zu kalt.
Leer ist der Korb,
doch immer noch schau ich mich um,
wenn ich – unschlüssig wohin – vors Haus trete.

KARA

Our little dog is dead.
No one lifts a head anymore
when I, unable to sleep,
haunt the kitchen at night.
In the woods no one
runs three steps ahead of me
to point out spots
worth pausing for,
the single oak, clumps of beeches
to be observed with pen and paper:
branches, trunks.

Swifter than my hasty thought,
more biddable than I could ever be,
more loyal than love itself demands,
was she, our little dog.
Never was the Baltic Sea
too cold for her – it was for me –
when I hurled the stick
far out into the listless waves.
The basket is empty
but still I look back
as – undecided where to go – I step outside the house.

DOPPELT IN DIE PILZE GEGANGEN

Auf Waldboden kam mir
mit scheinbar festem, dann aber
erkennbar tapsigem Schritt
jemand entgegen, der, gekleidet
in erdfarbenen Cord,
ich war, dem ich – tapsig in Cord –
näher und näher entgegenkam.
War gleich mir
mit schlechtziehender Pfeife
auf Waldboden unterwegs.

Beide zielstrebig. Runde Rücken.
Er an mir, ich an ihm wie achtlos vorbei.
Kurzer Blick nur aus Augenwinkeln.
Kein Erschrecken. Ich und ich
wollten nur wissen, wer mehr Pilze
in seinem Beutel heimtrug.


TWICE GONE MUSHROOMING

Across the forest floor someone
moved towards me with seemingly firm
then visibly clumsy steps,
someone who, clad
in earth-coloured cord,
was I myself, to whom I – clumsy in cord –
moved ever closer.
Was just like me
on his way across the forest floor,
his pipe drawing badly.

Both purposeful. Backs stooped.
He passing me and I him, almost casually.
Just brief glances out of the corner of the eye.
No alarm. I and I
only wanted to know who carried home
more mushrooms in his sack.

– Translations from the German by Hans-Christian Oeser

TRANSLATOR'S NOTE:

Günter Grass was born in Danzig (now Dansk) in 1927. With his first
novel *The Tin Drum* (1959) he achieved international acclaim. In 1999
he was awarded the Nobel Prize for Literature. Apart from many
other novels, plays, essays and speeches, he also published the poetry
collections (many of them with his own drawings) *Die Vorzüge der
Windhühner* (1956), *Gleisdreieck* (1960), *Ausgefragt* (1967), *Gesammelte
Gedichte* (1971), *Liebe geprüft* (1974), *Mit Sophie in die Pilze gegangen* (1976),
*Ach Butt, dein Märchen geht böse aus* (1983), *Die Gedichte 1955-1986* (1988),
*Tierschutz* (1990), *Novemberland. 13 Sonette* (1993) and *Fundsachen für
Nichtleser* (1997). *Selected Poems* came out in 1966, *In the Egg and Other
Poems* in 1977, both translated by Michael Hamburger and Christopher
Middleton. This selection, translated by Hans-Christian Oeser, is
taken from Grass's latest collection *Letzte Tänze* (2003), a sequence of
94 poems on dancing, coupling and death, and appears here for the
first time in English. With kind permission of Steidl Verlag, Göttingen.

## Gerard Smyth

THE ARTIST AS EULOGIST
*after Sean McSweeney*

The artist paints the ephemeral haze
of a sky in the west, works the spell that makes
the wetland pool a window to the underearth.

The artist as eulogist scans the landscape,
its tones and tints: nimbus, spindrift,
the mountain slope of rock and stone.

Like *those dark trees* Frost looked on
with worn-out eyes, the trees of Lissadell
are weather-beaten, Venetian red.

The artist needs to fill vast space
with bog-soil, shoreline, a native bloom
that leaves a native stain. The ground is rich,
damp with rain, the last ridge of light
blue as the welder's flame before it glimmers out.

## Gerard Smyth

GEOGRAPHER'S LANDSCAPE
*in memory of Dick Walsh*

I think of you as the man who followed the Danube
as far as the house of Elias Canetti.
A mystical quest that brought me once
to a city of bridges where women in headscarves
moved like a tribe keening
and shaking their wrist-bracelets.

In the opera house I tasted Hungarian wine,
woodwind came alive
during something by Bartók or Haydn.
In the central station I noticed
the allegorical formation of trains that were facing
the east and the west.

The piper's lament
you heard in Milltown Malbay was as ponderous
and melancholy as any Romanian rhapsody.
Yes, I think of you as the man
who followed the Danube: a journey of crossings
through the geographer's landscape.

## Hugh O'Donnell

A FINGER POINTING AT THE MOON
*in memoriam Fr D A Collins, murdered in South Africa, 16/11/02*

The right hand making up to the left
is how I remember them forming rabbits in silhouette,
(a smooch of light and shadow on the wall) –

remember my father's playing on the counterpane
in moonlight before she hunted them inside
for the night and tucked him in –

imagine Declan's folding into each other, just one
finger raised against the dipping knife, one
ear on the white-washed screen twitching.

## Louis Armand

BUCOLIC
*the weak vow of fidelity is formed by the cairn*

cut out with shears from the same
tooth-cloth; a maculated rag to
stuff a godless hole – blood sequins
threaded on a dressmaker's needle adorn
the dry carotid artery, whiter than
quicklime – night too has a way
of turning; a rusted faucet swollen by an
unremittant tide, pounding the sleepless
brain beyond culpability – there is
nothing left to fabricate or
confess: a slipknot, lead weight of the
boots, the trapper's jaw sunk
in a gulch beneath the wrecked hedge-
row – morning is the clotted felt
of a carcass gnawed by foxes, the scent of
wasted cartridges, the bitter aftertaste
of black tea

## Louis Armand

IMITATIONS ON A THEME

> *non ego divitias patrum fructusque requiro quos*
> *tulit antiquo condita messis auo*
> — Tibullus

bolt upright in that ancient
wedding dress white pleated on grey, as though
guessing already the decrepitude
that alone outlasted you – the cut-out
bridegroom holding a pair of gloves
in his right hand, an eye tilted
towards flanders – the cracked
oval picture frame which makes due remembrance
of all the schisms & excommunications...

but that house has long been emptied of your
arifacts. & when at last
the ceilings give up their pretence
& collapse once & for all, there'll be
no closeting with melancholy &
nostalgia – only the gradual demolition of
a husk even the weevils abandoned
with the first bad season – the old feeding grounds
blighted with insoluble contradictions

on such a scale nothing ever is resolved. gross
coincidence ennobled in the guise of
providence – pretended agent
of what the histories need not recount in its
obviousness. the strangeness is set aside
for more literary fancies:
hallucinatory landscapes of pointless
verdancy, untenanted allotments lorded over
by towers of grey intending rubble
defiant of nothing now but gravity

*Gosford Park, Co. Armagh*

# Eamon Grennan

STILL WAYFARING

Robert Lowell, *Collected Poems*, edited by Frank Bidart and David Gewanter, Faber and Faber, 2003, hb £40.

'I offer you my huddle of flesh and dismay', says Robert Lowell in a late poem. The line, as with so many of Lowell's, has a fraught, weighty feel to it, and is emblematic of its speaker – not only in the generously mannered 'offering' but also in the way the fact of flesh and the feeling of dismay are brought into alignment. In addition there is the unsparing modesty of 'huddle,' the way it reveals an unflinchingly lucid, uninflated sense of the self, as well as an undeceived clarity regarding what art can do as it tries to get the whole self, psychic warts and all, into focus, to bring the totality of consciousness within the scope of language. Lowell's brave persistence in this attempt places him among the most important poets of the twentieth century, both for his native strength and stature as well as for the nature of his influence on poets who followed him in America and elsewhere. Without him, any reading of the poetry of mid-century would be incomplete.

Odd then, that since his death in 1977 at the age of sixty, Lowell's presence in the poetic landscape has faded. Bishop and Plath are, for various reasons, more widely read, while Hughes, Larkin, Ginsberg and Ashbery command their respective audiences in a way Lowell has not. (Indeed it is difficult to say that Lowell has a specific 'audience' in the way the poets I've mentioned have). The appearance of this very hefty volume, however, with its nearly one thousand pages of text and almost two hundred pages of notes and other matter, should bring Lowell back into the prominence he deserves. It should establish him as the major American poet of his generation, important not just for the value of the work in itself, but exemplary in the coherent trajectory composed by his evolution as a poet, as he moved through a series of significant stylistic and substantive changes. (Like Yeats, Lowell's career is a series of powerful self-makings and unmakings as a poet, as a voice, as a style). Composing a constant, deliberate, but never mechanical design, this trajectory takes him from the early work (*Land of Unlikeness*, 1944, *Lord Weary's Castle*, 1946, and *The Mills of the Kavanaughs*, 1951), through the powerful first phase of a middle period (beginning with the breakthrough 1959 volume, *Life Studies*, and continuing with the two magisterially accomplished collections, *For the Union Dead* in 1964, and *Near the Ocean* in 1967), and proceeding then into the second phase of the middle period, consisting of the remarkable series of unrhymed blank verse sonnets gathered into separate volumes as, initially, *Notebook* (1970), and further amplified and painstakingly revised into the three volumes that appeared in 1973 – *History, For Lizzie and Harriet*, and *The Dolphin*. After this extraordinary harvest of poems charting the inner and outer life of the poet, giving concrete, stabilising form to an embattled but always active consciousness at once public and private, there is another stylistic swerve into the single volume that is all we have of a 'late' phase. *Day By Day* (which appeared in the year of his death) is, however, a suitably autumnal collection, embodying another shift of ambition, another way for the poet to inhabit, populate, and record his world. In its unevenness, its apparent feeling about for a new way, this volume might in fact be called a prologue to a final phase, a prologue whose summary formulation might be in the poem called, ironically enough, 'Epilogue': so much of the muted ambition of this last collection might be summed up in the single emblematic line, 'Yet why not say what happened?' In addition to these volumes, and expanding the shape they make, there is the collection of idiosyncratic translations, *Imitations* (1961), which remains a vital and revealing segment of the Lowell oeuvre.

Between them, these volumes inscribe the coherent arc of an evolving imagination, more distinct in its shape than that composed by the career of any other poet of his generation. Even the work of his two strongest American contemporaries, Bishop and Berryman, or that of the younger Plath, when each is taken as a whole, does not achieve the same fullness of design. It might be argued that one has to go back to Yeats to see such a coherence of developing imagination, such a deliberate power of poetic change, such a decisive shaping of the poetic career, or to see how the poet shapes the poetry to fit the unfolding scheme, with all its minute accidental particularities, of the life.

The sheer weight and achievement of this career becomes all the more impressive when we realise it was composed in the face of a life tortured and made tumultuous by recurrent bouts of mental illness – his manic depression compounded by alcohol – that had harrowing effects on Lowell and on those close to him, chief among them his three wives and chief among these his second wife, Elizabeth Hardwick, (outside whose New York apartment Lowell died, of heart failure (an 'enlarged heart'), sitting in a taxi and clutching a portrait of his third wife, Caroline Blackwood, whom he had just left in Ireland.

By making Lowell's life in poetry available to us in this massive volume, and thereby letting the true stature of the poet emerge beyond argument, Frank Bidart (a younger, close friend of Lowell's, and himself an important extender of Lowell's poetic territory), and David Gewanter have performed an invaluable service to American poetry and poetry in general. While no one except a reviewer is likely to read through the whole enormous volume at a sitting (or a fortnight's sittings), it is the container of all we need in order to see Lowell's achievement for what it was and is, one of the richest and most vigorous and most complete in modern poetry.

After this general comment, I should get a little closer to particulars, to see exactly how Lowell made his 'huddle of flesh and dismay' endure, be a recognizable and enlarging way into the world. A brief sample from each phase of his poetic development may lend some particularity to the general picture. Here's the concluding passage of 'The Quaker Graveyard in Nantucket', from *Lord Weary's Castle*. (*Land of Unlikeness* was Lowell's first collection, but he never reprinted it, and it appears as an Appendix in the *Collected Poems*).

> Atlantic, you are fouled with the blue sailors,
> Sea-monsters, upward angel, downward fish:
> Unmarried and corroding, spare of flesh,
> Mart once of supercilious, wing'd clippers,
> Atlantic, where your bell-trap guts its spoil
> You could cut the brackish winds with a knife
> Here in Nantucket, and cast up the time
> When the Lord God formed man from the sea's slime
> And breathed into his face the breath of life,
> And blue-lung'd combers lumbered to the kill.
> The Lord survives the rainbow of His will.

What is immediately obvious here is the rhythmically muscular, slightly gnarled grandiloquence of the iambic pentameter couplets, the solidity of the vocabulary, the impersonal authority of the voice, the tense control of the curving syntactical period, the way line and sentence wind sinuously around each other. The voice is large, loud, declarative, exclamatory. The speaker seems to be a spokesman for something (a something that remains obscure, though connected with the condition of religious faith in a world of violent action) rather than a biographically particular personality. It is a style of enlarged commentary, at once physical, intellectual and dramatic. It deals in large-scale generalities, a world of universal truths enfolded in vivid, significance-bearing images. Standing behind it are the oddly consorting shades of Milton, Hopkins, and Lowell's early master, Allen Tate. It risks being overdone, musclebound, being impressive rather than accessible, though 'You could cut the brackish winds with a knife' has a lovely, spoken actuality, and although it would be hard to deny, in lines like the last two, the genuine power of this buoyantly lyrical verbal music. Such a passage carries evidence of what Lowell himself called 'the symbols and heroics of my first book.' It reveals a poet steeped in and speaking out of the tradition, the whole linguistic and rhythmic heft of which is his persona. After experiencing such qualities, a passage from a poem in *Life Studies* – comes as a shock (as it did to its first readers, in 1959):

> Tamed by *Miltown*, we lie on Mother's bed;
> the rising sun in war paint dyes us red;
> in broad daylight her gilded bed-posts shine
> abandoned, almost Dionysian.
> At last the trees are green on Marlborough Street,
> blossoms on our magnolia ignite
> the morning with their murderous five-days' white.
> All night I've held your hand,
> as if you had
> a fourth time faced the kingdom of the mad –
> its hackneyed speech, its homicidal eye –
> and dragged me home alive. . . Oh my *Petite*,
> clearest of all God's creatures, still all air and nerve…
>
> – from 'Man and Wife'

Gone is the drama of verbal gesture. In its place is an attempt to get down the facts, both objective and subjective. Narrative replaces melo-drama, but the narrative is not Miltonic, it is an artfully orchestrated biographical record. The voice is personal, implicated, in the world, not that of a rhetorically elevated commentator. The new style, however – less the poetry of confession than of crystallization – is not without its formal bracings (in its couplets and iambics, in a verse line that shuttles to and from the pentameter), nor is it without its verbal eloquence, its exclamatory energy. Behind this might lie, indeed, the Milton of 'Lycidas' (a poem much admired by Lowell), with its musical movement of long and short lines, its fluid rhyming. What is happening poetically here, though, is new: autobiographical in a direct way, it does not lose the dignities of form, yet it does not use these formal features to inflate or evade the issue: it seeks truth, by being true in its own aesthetically responsible way to the facts of the matter. His candour, as Frank Bidart says, 'is an illusion created by art.' The self has come into play, uttering itself in a voice that is speaking, not declaiming. Such a speaking voice is in part a result (Lowell himself said) of his reading his poems aloud at events on the West Coast, where, as he says, 'I began to have a certain disrespect for the tight forms.' In performance, he found himself softening their slightly muscle-bound qualities; he heard what Ginsberg and the Beats were doing in their own way, and he learned to loosen up and lighten up.

Having absorbed these lessons, Lowell proceeds in both his next two books to exert a more deliberately formal power on this loosened and more personal style, producing such great poems in rhymed stanzas as the brilliant 'For the Union Dead' and 'Waking Early Sunday Morning', as well as some powerful pieces in variously shaped rhyming or free verse strophes. As he said of the poems in *For the Union Dead*, he wanted to achieve 'some music and elegance and splendor, but not in any programmatic sense.' In so many of the poems in both volumes, what peers corrosively through the matter is Lowell's power as a melancholy elegist, spiked with dashes of startling, edgy, physically immediate imagery. What we are aware of is a poet excruciatingly alert to himself and his surroundings – as in 'Returning':

> Yet sometimes I catch my vague mind
> circling with a glazed eye
> for a name without a face, or a face without a name,
> and at every step,
> I startle them. They start up,
> dog-eared, bald as baby birds.

In such poems he has found a language to deal without flinching with the bare, unromanticised facts, a language tense with the electric energy of its own awareness, bristling with what Randall Jarrell called 'the singular thingness of every being in the world.' In addition, he moves between private reminiscences and revelations (carried over from *Life Studies*) and the larger realm of portraiture, public action and response. These poems register the link between consciousness and conscience, and register – as a nervous system registers the stresses of joy, sorrow, uncertainty, pain – the constant shift and nuance of the relationship between them. The effect of mixing public and private is never more magisterially accomplished than in these magnificent opening and closing stanzas (their eight-line octosyllabic couplets borrowed from Marvell, their randomly iambic measure his own) from what has to be one of his very greatest poems, 'Waking Early Sunday Morning':

> O to break loose, like the chinook
> salmon jumping and falling back,
> nosing up to the impossible
> stone and bone-crushing waterfall –
> raw-jawed, weak-fleshed there, stopped by ten
> steps of the roaring ladder, and then
> to clear the top on the last try,
> alive enough to spawn and die.

[...]

Pity the planet, all joy gone
from this sweet volcanic cone;
peace to our children when they fall
in small war on the heels of small
war – until the end of time
to police the earth, a ghost
orbiting forever lost
in our monotonous sublime.

Not since Yeats, I suspect, could such a marriage of private and political feeling be accomplished in verse at once so resonantly public and so feelingly intimate, so capable of using at once the first person singular and plural, while at the same time achieving such a panoptic view of the whole human picture. His vision is stereoscopic: one eye on the self, the other on the big picture. So, as a poet, he lives in a perpetual lightning storm of significance.

Lowell's next poetic step, or swerve, was into the astonishing enterprise of his blank verse sonnets, hundreds of them accumulating over a few years, published between 1969 and 1973. What this great avalanche of poems aspires to, it seems to me, is to be somehow a response or rival to Pound's *Cantos*. As Pound defined the epic as 'a poem containing history', so Lowell – after first publishing the poems in what he himself called the rather 'jumbled' *Notebook* – revised and rearranged most of the sonnets under the title, *History*, reserving the more intimate familial pieces for the volumes *For Lizzie and Harriet*. (*The Dolphin*, more sonnets, came later). 'History' here, in spite of the presence of actual historical figures and facts, means personal history, a history of what this single consciousness had encountered and how it had responded. Poems do not form a narrative sequence, but are radial, radiating out from this centre of compulsively active emotional cerebration. In its radial rather than linear manner the collection breaks down the notion of history itself as a continuous narrative, but demonstrates how discontinuity, reversal, and surprise in themselves generate 'design.' Fourteen lines by fourteen lines – each as vigorous and speedy and unpredictable as that chinook salmon nosing its way up the impossible – it is a radical record of a consciousness, its public and private zones, its modes of feeling, its manners of judge-ment, its casts of opinion; all the coruscating moral, physical, and emotional zones are given their due. The poems, too, move among voices, as the speaker abdicates any notion of supreme authority, and willingly lets others, whether personae in his private drama or larger voices on the public stage, have their say. (In this, as in some of the earlier 'voice' poems, Lowell joins Eliot and Pound as a knowing heir of that greatest of dramatic monologists, Robert Browning). While not every one of the sonnets is a winner, the sheer abundance is staggering, each one a 'moment's monument' to some flash of memory, or instant of immediate feeling, or some braced and sharpened moral judgement. Among the great and greatly useful array of notes appended to this edition are a number of Lowell's own remarks about the enterprise. Calling the sonnets 'unrhymed, loose blank-verse stanzas,' he says they 'can say almost anything conversation or correspondence can. These poems mix the day to day with history...always the instant, sometimes changing to the lost... written quickly... Words came rapidly, almost four hundred sonnets in four years – a calendar of workdays. I did nothing but write... Ideas sprang from the bushes, my head... I wished to describe the immediate instant...Things I felt or saw, or read were drift in the whirlpool, the squeeze of the sonnet and the loose ravel of blank verse.' No amount of quoting will do justice to the sheer abundance of the whole enterprise. Here is a touch from 'Ezra Pound,' simply recording speech, but in doing so limning a sharp pen-portrait

> You showed me your blotched, bent hands, saying, 'Worms.
> When I talked that nonsense about Jews on the Rome
> wireless, Olga knew it was shit, and still loved me.'
> And I, 'Who else has been in Purgatory?'
> You, 'I began with a swelled head and end with swelled feet.'

And here is a sonnet called 'Seals', from *For Lizzie and Harriet*, which – in its simplicity of yearning and its scrupulous adherence to its chosen image – manages to be what Lowell hoped his verse would be: 'heartbreaking':

> If we must live again, not us; we might
> go into seals, we'd handle ourselves better:
> able to dawdle, able to torpedo,
> all too at home in our three elements,
> ledge, water and heaven – if man could restrain his hand. . .
> We flipper the harbor, blots and patches and oilslick,
> so much bluer than water, we think it sky.
> Creature could face creator in this suit,
> fishers of fish not men. Some other August,
> the easy seal might say, 'I could not sleep
> last night; suddenly I could write my name. . . .'
> Then all seals, preternatural like us,
> would take direction, head north – their haven
> green ice in a greenland never grass.

What such a poem shows is the grace, vulnerability and power all locked up in the one consciousness as it achieves exact, balanced, fluent expression. Indeed, from a study of such a poem, from a close reading of the whole remarkable enterprise represented by these three collections, I think any young poet could, in purely stylistic terms, learn an enormous amount – from their ability to be at once loose and well-braced, from their caesuras, enjambments, line/sentence choreography, from the way they play so many rhythmic variations on the form without ever seeming monotonous or repetitious. In them, I'd say, we see a poet working at the top of his bent, able almost effortlessly it seems, to weave his ordinary life into verse, packing it with allusive matter and matter of the moment. And he manages to do this while, at his best, never letting it seem overstuffed: the form carries it all, sustains it, holds things in their right equilibrium, the way they are held in the fluid consciousness of our lives. These sonnets, at once so personal and so objectively persuasive of the truth of their moment, are one of the twentieth century's best monuments to the poetry of subjective response, the meditative lyricism of consciousness descending in an odd line from not only *The Prelude* and *The Cantos*, but also from the great 'Conversation poems' of Coleridge and (in their attachment to the quotidian in a normative speaking voice) from the work of William Carlos Williams.

Such poems as are collected in these three volumes of 1973 are effectively a day by day accounting of the flashing life of consciousness itself, caught in flight, stabilised into these kinetic packages of fourteen lines (a form we should probably call the 'American sonnet'). Lowell's last collection, then, chooses the phrase 'day by day' as its title. In it, after another radical shift of style, he assembles poems that pay another kind of tribute to passing, quotidian, ordinary facts and actions. Unlike the flashing compactness of the sonnets, these poems are loose-limbed, lacking that earlier intensity ('gone now the sonnet's cramping and military beat' was how Lowell himself put it). I find myself at times regretting the lack, and lamenting the way some of them seem to emerge out of material not only private but too trivial to interest a stranger. On reflection, though, what one can detect in these poems is the poet's search for a language, a mode of poetic speech, adequate to a condition of consciousness at lower voltage. And there are moments of a new kind of power, the power not of shaping but of merely acknowledging. The language is trying to find its feet in a world of pure response, response in which the very notion of 'authority' is held up for inspection and found wanting. Short lines dawdling down the page are a way to register, it seems, a state of watchful, quieted sobriety, as in the sad piece 'For John Berryman', for Lowell's friend and rival, a rueful memory allied to a recognition of a present without the old electricity in it:

Do you wake dazed like me,
and find your lost glasses in a shoe?

Something so heavy lies on my heart –
there, still here, the good days
when we sat by a cold lake in Maine,
talking about the *Winter's Tale*,

Leontes' jealousy
in Shakespeare's broken syntax.
You got there first....

Girls will not frighten the frost from the grave.

There is a summary aspect to this book, a sort of paying of debts of memory, as well as a sort of undriven, seemingly undirected contemplativeness, stopping now on reminiscence, now on a love poem, now on a casually rendered landscape. What it suggests, often, is a desultory looking around for subjects, the poet in a curious fix, in a kind of becalmed state, as here at the conclusion of 'Ants':

I lie staring under an old oak,
stubby, homely, catacombed by ants,
more of a mop than a tree.
I fear the clumsy boughs will fall.
Is its weak, wooden heart strong enough
to bear my weight if I should climb
from knob to knob to the top?
How uneasily I am myself,
as a child I found the sky too close.
Why am I childish now and ask
for daffy days when I tried to read
*Walden*'s ant-war aloud to you for love?

And yet the poetic victory implicit in this collection is the way Lowell turns this very state of becalmed looking about into the prompt to his next phase, a phase in which he will not try to *make* anything out of his material, simply let it be itself, be truly 'imagined' (by which he means something like Keats must have meant by 'negative capability') and in being itself to discover, not contrive, its meaning. It is an insight, formal as well as substantive, that stands on the verge of fresh revelations, is the necessary prologue to a fresh swerve of imaginative energy into language. The possibilities of this phase, which he never lived to properly inhabit or

explore, are formulated (or, better, adumbrated) once and for all in
'Epilogue':

> Those blessed structures, plot and rhyme –
> why are they no help to me now
> I want to make
> something imagined, not recalled?
>
> [...]
> Yet why not say what happened?
> Pray for the grace of accuracy
> Vermeer gave to the sun's illumination
> stealing like a tide across a map
> to his girl solid with yearning.
> We are poor passing facts,
> warned by that to
> give each figure in the photograph
> his living name.

This is to be his last word on the subject, and it seems (in a way that
reminds me, in spite of its completely different tonality and outcome, of
Yeats's 'The Circus Animals Desertion') like a wryly rueful admission of
failure. But another, more encompassing truth is that Lowell had in one
way or another spent his whole life as a poet responding to 'poor passing
facts' and searching out at each fresh swerve and phase of his too short
poetic life the living names. His whole career, which for all its swings
and roundabouts is all of an evolving piece, is an attempt to 'say what
happened' while keeping faith with the happening, being faithful to the
language. And while it may not always have been Vermeer's, there is a
'grace of accuracy' in all his best work, accuracy to a consciousness that
remains true to the language, to poetry, and to the self (no matter how
ramshackle or poor its 'passing facts'). This is his legacy, the value of
which is what the *Collected Poems* puts beyond question. Once Lowell
had abandoned Catholicism (which he converted to in 1940 and left in
1948) he sought no myth to give meaning to the random shapes his life
created as he lived it. But as a poet he stayed faithful and responsible to
each of these shapes, no matter how contradictory. ('We must live our
own contradictions without evasions,' says a favourite poet of his,
Montale), attempting, with a seriousness and a continuous effort to give
– in the picture that his own consciousness gave back of the world –
each figure its proper name.
With its rich compendium of useful notes, some of them containing
early drafts of poems, this big book is an invaluable addition to our

understanding not only of Lowell himself but also of twentieth-century poetry in English, on the map of which he is a major feature (a feature whose influence is palpable on such Irish poets as John Montague, Seamus Heaney in his later work and, most potently, Derek Mahon). Having put his figure back in the picture, this collection will soon spawn, I hope, a new *Selected Poems*. Easily portable, I imagine that such a volume – in readers new to Lowell (and for those older readers for whom he has slipped below the radar of contemporary critical attention) – would generate something of the excitement we had as students in the Sixties, when we read *Life Studies* for the first time. We were dazzled then by the sound of a voice speaking a language we could understand, a language both traditional and risky, the sound of a voice – true to the self and true to what we knew of poetry – making sense in the world, and winning, as his biographer, Ian Hamilton has said, 'a major expansion of the territory of poetry.' And these sentiments were only intensified when we read *For the Union Dead* and *Near the Ocean*. What we were hearing was the sound of a new master, something our ears were hungry for, the sound of a voice we recognised for the affecting, tormented, sceptical, plangent, and heartbreaking thing it was. What this *Collected Poems* tells us, thankfully, is that we weren't wrong. When Lowell looked at the *Selected Poems* that came out in 1977 (and is out of print), he described it as 'a small-scale Prelude, written in many different styles and with digressions, yet a continuing story – still wayfaring.' The *Collected Poems* shows the whole of that 'continuing story,' and shows just how ceaseless and steady and courageous this particular wayfarer was. A new *Selected* would increase and broaden the audience. 'We are things,' he said, 'thrown in the air / alive in flight.' It might be a description of his own poems: alive, and in flight. But earthbound too, living among the grounded creatures, the turtle he wrote about, or the creature at the end of 'Skunk Hour,' a creature he looked at with that mesmerised attention he had learned from Elizabeth Bishop (who made, he said, 'the casual perfect') :

> I stand on top
> of our back steps and breathe the rich air –
> a mother skunk with her column of kittens swills the garbage pail.
> She jabs her wedge-head in a cup
> of sour cream, drops her ostrich tail,
> and will not scare.

In the end this may be his best emblem (with another hint in it, maybe, of 'The Circus Animals' Desertion'): the poet fully taking in the world, its rich air and its cast-off garbage, with a tenacity of purpose, exhilaration even, and a hunger that will not be denied.

# Ian Duhig

## THE IRISH BOOMERANG

This piece, along with Peter Didsbury's, were given as talks at a seminar on 'Poets and the North of England' held in Trinity College Dublin, where Ian Duhig was International Writer Fellow in association with the British Council for 2003.

When I first began thinking about an event to celebrate cultural links between the Republic of Ireland and the North of England, Gerald Dawe – who I would now like to thank for all the planning and effort he put into making this happen – asked me what I would call it. I found this incredibly difficult. The content was presenting no problem: there are multiple connections between the poetry, music and novels (see Brendan Kennelly's *The Florentines*) of the two areas, but a name?

I canvassed my friends to receive such helpful suggestions as *Riverclogdance* and *Micks in the Sticks*. In the end, as you will see from our posters, we opted for no clear title. One humorous suggestion which was considered seriously was *The Irish Boomerang*, after the old joke. The Irish Boomerang differed from its Australian counterpart in that when you threw it, it didn't come back – it only sang about coming back.

And it is in the realm of song that I want to pursue an analogy with poetry. This evening you will hear a considerable variety of poetry from the North of England, and some personal reflections from Peter Didsbury on certain aspects of the relationships with Ireland as they have seemed important to him. However, the point I am trying to make is simple: the impact of poetry from the Republic of Ireland on the North of England is quite literally incalculable. There are obvious areas of influence, such as that of Yeats on the young Larkin; Robert Graves on Ted Hughes, although perhaps more particularly with relation to Graves's *The White Goddess*; that of Nuala Ní Dhomhnaill (paradoxically a Lancashire lass by birth: this knife cuts both ways) on such northern women poets as Ann Sansom. If I say all of this is incalculable, how can I hope to trace its extent? I hope to do so by virtue of an analogy with the traditional music of the areas, starting with the late eighteenth century, when Irish migration to her self-appointed mother country came to be marked.

The poet John Clare, a folklorist and fiddler like his father before him, wrote of getting tunes from 'The Irish drovers on the road', while in Yorkshire the annual influx for harvesting were called 'The July Barbers', which is also the title of a song about them by Mike Harding. But as the Enclosure gained pace, they were joined by itinerant English.

In her *The Irish Contribution to English Traditional Music*, Francesca Allinson writes that English folksong during this period altered in style because it became 'saturated' – her word – with Irish melody[1]. The technicalities of the process are described by Samuel Bayard[2]; contrasting the English and Irish melody styles he writes:

> The English style is characterised by a certain solidity of melodic build and emphasis throughout the tune of the strong notes of the mode, like the tonic or dominant tones, and by preference for the sort of melodic movement which 'get somewhere' which is not held up by hesitating progression or undue overlay of ornamental features... The English singer's leaning to relatively straightforward and simple melodic lines is counteracted in Irish tradition by love of ornament, of multiplying notes, of varying rhythmic patterns by this sort of multiplication.

This same ornamental tendency, Bayard believes, gives to Irish music a 'wavering and unemphatic movement', with a habit of lingering on certain notes or tones, in 'repeating them before going on to another tone, thus impeding the course of the melody'. Further to this, in A L Lloyd's *Folk Song in England*, Lloyd writes that

> Bayard's description of the English style is neatly apt for the tunes of our older tradition, but our later tradition shows a great, perhaps preponderant number of melodies that fit his Irish characterisation.[3]

Numerous tunes and songs such as 'Blackwater Side' in the nineteenth century attest to this process continuing, but so as not to impede my own onward course I want to take my story up to Darach Ó Catháin, the Connemara *sean nós* exponent who lived and sang in Leeds from the 60s until his death. However, in terms of my analogy here, I would like to suggest that Bayard's 'wavering and unemphatic movement', his remarks about the Irish love of ornament, of certain notes repeated before going on to another, 'thus impeding the onward course of the melody', of what Lloyd describes as 'enchanting hesitancies', 'hovering mysteries', and 'meandering qualities' – these are all expressions that could be applied to a thick thread of Irish literature in the English language that runs through Laurence Sterne and Oscar Wilde, on to Flann O'Brien and Paul Muldoon.

In an unpublished poem, Kavanagh writes of despair as 'an illness like winter alone in Leeds' and while Kavanagh never visited Leeds, someone who knew the true bite of a line like that was Darach Ó Catháin. Darach came to the city which is now my home in search of work from the base of the large Irish community that settled here from the 19th century – if I had time I would like to discuss the nineteenth century socialist firebrand and poet Tom Maguire who came to Leeds from Ireland, a practical activist and force behind the successful gas workers' strike in the city, who now has a road through a local cemetery named after him. Darach was in the opinion of Seán Ó Riada the greatest Connemara *sean nós* singer of his generation. He was a friend to Irish poets in Leeds such as Brendan Kennelly and Pearse Hutchinson, both of them enjoying the opportunity to speak Irish, but Darach's life was harder than those that poets lead nowadays. Nevertheless he was held in high esteem by the large Irish music community in Leeds, through which I got to know about Darach and hear him sing from time to time. I believe that some of these performances surpassed any of the recordings I have heard: Darach might sing looking close and deep into someone's eyes, or holding their hand to his forehead. The thing it reminded me of most was Lorca's description of *duende* in 'canto jondo' (or 'deep song') in the Flamenco tradition, where *duende* (meaning something like 'goblin' or malevolent spirit), describes – as in the Blues – how the raw suffering of the singer's experience breaks through into their art, taking it beyond art. Darach didn't know Spanish but his performances certainly had *duende*. His family life was difficult, although he had a wonderful relationship with his disabled son, but the world stopped to hear him sing. It was listening to Darach that I understood something in Lloyd's book, where he related the impact of Irish styles on English song to the progress of the Enclosure. I had thought Lloyd was merely being a good communist and returning our attention to the means of production. But I really feel his point was that while so many people from the poorer levels of the host society were being turned off the land and out of their homes, they found something for themselves in traditional Irish music: its great superiority in expressing grief. Similarly Bayard's comments on the Irish love of ornament 'impeding the onward course of the melody' made sense: we all know what is the only end of song.

Nowadays, aficionados speak of 'the Leeds style' of playing traditional Irish music. This is distinguished, as you can imagine, by a highly-ornamental treatment of the tune – perhaps under the influence of Darach's style. In fact, not only do you hear about a Leed's style but in bands like 'Cúig', the fiddler Paul Ruane is described in the press as having a 'Leeds/Sligo' style; similarly there is a 'Mayo/Leeds' style, recognising the contribution of immigrants from that county to the Yorkshire city.

I have heard some grumbling from members of the English traditional music community in Yorkshire, and it is true that in many venues where you also heard English folk music now you only hear Irish. It is further true that a lot of English traditional musicians have begun playing Irish music for professional reasons – an example would be Gordon Tyrrell. A sensitive interpreter of his own heritage, he became more well known for accompanying Irish musicians on tour, such as the piper Leon Rowsome, son of the more famous Leo Rowsome, who appeared in the film *Playboy of the Western World*, scored by Seán Ó Riada.

In a larger sense in England, Irish music somehow represents all folk music. For example, it was a background music there for an advert for the Scottish Tourist Board; it is frequently used to suggest early English rural scenes on programmes such as 'Time Team', while on the Sky History Channel it might feature on the sound track for anywhere in the world in the past to symbolise rustic purity and an innocent culture – you can even hear its influence on the music of the hobbits in the first instalment of Peter Jackson's *Lord of the Rings* trilogy of films. Again, what I would like to suggest is that the dominance Irish music has attained in the last 30 to 40 years in England and elsewhere is closely analogous to the dominance attained by Irish poetry in English during exactly the same period.

Finally, I would like to end by using my own circumstances as an example of how traditional music in England, including Irish traditional music, can influence a contemporary poet in unexpected ways. I used to run a hostel for homeless people in York that was built next door to a pub famous for its folk music presentations, with acts which included the likes of Paul Brady, recently from Planxty at the time. However, when the landlord found out what we were opening next door, he barred all staff and residents of the hostel with immediate and permanent effect. Like some of my customers, I have been barred from pubs in the past myself, just not normally before I actually got there. Exquisite insult was added to injury on folk nights when on shift you had to listen to them next door belting out songs like 'Sullivan's John' and 'I Am a Jolly Beggar-man' and other renditions of life on the open road. The irony was suffocating.

In time, I started setting some of the stories of the people I worked with to the tunes that were coming through the wall. I would like to finish with one of these, a poem about a young woman at the hostel. As a literary and musical audience you might not know that in England if social workers want to take a child into care, and the mother seems to be avoiding them, they will come to pick up the child when they think everybody is at home sleeping.

Notes:
1. Francesca Allinson, *The Irish Contribution to English Traditional Tunes*.
2. Samuel Bayard, 'The Principal Melodic Families' in *The Critics and the Ballad*.
3. A L Lloyd, *Folksong in England*.

Ian Duhig

COME THE MORNING
(Air: 'The Trees They Do Grow High')

As the trees lose all their leaves
Evenings close round me
And I think when all the dreams that's passed
Since my young man I seen,
Now I must make my bed
In the crook of this blind lane
With a bonny boy, who's young, but who's growing.

When we were both fifteen
With him I fell in love;
The morning of his sixteenth year
I delivered him a son;
Before my man was seventeen
On his grave the grass grew green –
Pure heroin buried him, now he's growing.

They brought my love a shroud
Of the oriental brown;
For each needle's stitch I found in it
O a tear it did run down;
Who once I kissed so hungrily
Kissed the night below,
Not his own flesh and blood, nor sees him growing.

They came to take my baby
In the middle of the night;
'It's for the best' one bastard said
And I'm sure that she was right.
O I'd never walk these streets alone
Now I walk these streets alone.
I've forgotten all your names come the morning.

# Peter Didsbury

A FIRE SHARED

When I was asked to write something for this event, my instinct was to refuse. I doubted that I has anything particularly relevant to say. However, Ian Duhig assured me that I could wander as far from the stated theme as I liked, so I agreed to give it a go. It may be that in a few minutes' time you will wish I had stuck to my guns. But this remains to be seen.

I decided to approach the task as I would a poem. By starting with some image or fact which excited me, and then seeing where it would lead. By the end of that Saturday afternoon, the inevitable had happened – I'd produced a new poem but was still no nearer having any prose to set before you.

Or so I thought, until it occurred to me that I might simply talk about the materials out of which this new poem had arisen, and then end by reading it. Which is what I shall now do.

The starting point was something that had cropped up in conversation with Ian: the fact that there is a surprising number of references, in eighteenth- and nineteenth-century writing, to the Irish language being heard on English streets. They're casual, incidental, seemingly offhand, but can carry quite a disproportionate charge. A large but usually submerged Irish component within English society fleetingly breaks the surface.

There's an essay by Leigh Hunt called 'Bricklayers, and an Old Book'. It opens with a powerful vignette of the parched brickfields and building plots of an expanding early nineteenth-century London. Noon on a baking August day. The sudden chink of a trowel against a brick. And then, down a nearby ladder,

> comes dancing, with hod on shoulder, a bricklayer, who looks as dry as
> his vocation – his eyes winking, his mouth gaping; his beard grim with a
> week's growth, the rest of his hair like a badger's.

There follows a rapid descent into slapstick, in which reader and author, startled out of gentlemanly reverie, get splashed with lime being mixed in a nearby puddle, then stumble into the milky but caustic waters. Contemporary fears, diffused by comedy, are quietly articulated in the conclusion to the scene:

> Finally, your shoe is burned; and as the bricklayer says something to his
> fellow in Irish, who laughs, you fancy that he is witty at your expense,
> and has made some ingenious bull.

There's a latent anxiety here about the stranger in one's midst, undoubt-
edly, but the portrait is not otherwise unsympathetic. The bricklayer is
accorded a Devil-may-care, if potentially dangerous, presence. It contrasts
sharply, for example, with cartoon portraits of Irish labourers later in the
century; Paddy or Mick as a shambling creature with vacant expression
and, almost unfailingly, a jutting upper lip exaggerated almost into a
beak. At least here the grim apparition comes 'dancing' down the ladder,
and his foreign witticism is fully expected to have been ingenious.

But this is not a sociological essay, just an attempt to peer into the
continuum out of which the poem was born. Hunt's essay brought to
mind a more local literary notice, which has long haunted my imagination.
And here, at last, we come to the North of England.

My own home of Hull, like many other towns in England in the sum-
mer of 1849, was devastated by an outbreak of Asiatic cholera. Upwards
of two thousand people perished in three months, and an account of the
outbreak by a contemporary clergyman, James Sibree[1], is replete with
Dante-esque horror. The urgency of mortality was such that grave-pits
to hold between ten and twenty coffins apiece had to be dug. The streets
at night were lit by flaming tar barrels, in the light of which urgent
relatives went in search of doctors, undertakers and priests. The town's
recently built General Cemetery, of which it was inordinately proud (and
in which Larkin would one day be filmed chatting to Betjeman) was con-
stantly thronged and often less than orderly:

> The whole scene was sometimes revolting to the mourners, and only
> added to their grief. Besides this, there was, at times, much confusion,
> and other sounds than the chaplain's voice in committing the bodies of
> the deceased to the ground. The Irish women would come, and falling
> down on the graves of their dead, howl out, in their native tongue, the
> 'death wail', and no effort on the part of our men could restrain them.

A lack of decorum, indeed. But that is not the point I wish to make, and
time is running out. These long-dead Irishwomen in Hull General
Cemetery, just down the road from where I live, affect me with a powerful
sense of loss – their own loss, naturally, but also that of a language and
culture. They are hardly noticed in accounts of the nineteenth-century
town, until tragedy brings them into focus almost as graveside accessories,
with horribly exotic and troubling ululations. And yet, Hull had a surpris-
ingly large Irish population at the time. The 1851 Census shows that 3,000
out of 95,000 inhabitants of Hull and the adjacent villages had actually
been born in Ireland. If we add second-generation children to this total,
then the Irish population of the town itself may well have been in excess
of 5%. They were largely poor and, like their English counterparts, with

whom they lived cheek-by-jowl, occupied squalid courtyard and tenement housing, where families of four or more would occupy a single room. There were other similarities with the English poor, who were also in the process of being sundered from a rich oral culture. I may mention here, since it figures in the poem, the Yorkshire *bargeist*, or 'bear-ghost', a distinctly unpleasant supernatural entity straight out of the German forests, yet known to have been prowling the streets of Hull well into the nineteenth century.

And that's about it, really. What cross-cultural or personal contacts obtained between the two communities I'm not equipped to judge. I'm sure it would be possible, for example, to examine the Irish contribution to Hull's radicalism, but this is not my task. The day-to-day articulation of sympathy is necessarily lost, and the meeting I imagine in this poem is but an elegiac possibility. It's called 'A Fire Shared'.

1. James Sibree, *Fifty Years' Recollections of Hull; or half-a-century of public life and ministry*. Hull, 1884.

**Peter Didsbury**

A FIRE SHARED

This evening I have spent
in the Irishwoman's room.
A fire shared is a fire cheaper.

A twelvemonth since
I knew her not at all.
Our hearths were crowded then
but now it is fitting
that one of them bides cold.
A fire shared is a fire cheaper by far.

She has enough English now
for January tales
of our slavering *bargeist*,
which stalks these dark flagged yards
intent on the taking of children.
She would not have understood a year ago.

A year ago her English was just enough
for blessing or cursing,
to ask the price of bread
or directions to a pump.
But now a fire shared
is a fine instructive tutor.

She has enough English now
to match my *bargeists* and goblins
with *pookas* and suchlike,
and I find I have learned what these are,
from many a night
spent sharing and cheapening fire.

A twelvemonth ago I would not have known
the Irish for 'sorrow', 'cholera', 'children',
or who stood by me at the same wide grave-mouth
as we wept after each of our fashions.
But now I know these things,
which are things I have learned

in the school of the ruined hearth,
which is held in both our rooms,
where a fire shared
is the cheapest fire of all.

## Peter Robinson in conversation with Peter Carpenter

When Peter Robinson's first collection, *Overdrawn Account*, was published in 1980 he was described by a critic in the *PN Review* as 'in my judgement the finest poet of his generation.' His first Carcanet collection, *This Other Life*, won the Cheltenham Prize in 1988 and was described by *The Guardian* as 'a major event'. According to another critic, 'Robinson is the finest poet alive when it comes to the probing of shifts in atmosphere, momentary changes in the weather of the mind, each poem an astonishingly finely-tuned gauge for recording the pressures and processes that generate lived occasions.' In 2003 Carcanet published his *Selected Poems*. Peter Robinson was born in 1953 in the north of England and since 1989 he has taught literature in Japan where he lives with his wife and their two daughters. His work as a translator includes *Selected Poems of Vittorio Sereni* (Anvil Press, with Marcus Perryman) and *The Great Friend and Other Translated Poems*, published in 2002 by Peter Carpenter's Worple Press.

**Peter Carpenter**: *Many of your poems over the years have dealt with a sense of 'displacement' or being on the edge of things, not least due to the situation that you described in the note for* Anywhere You Like. *'I have grown more used to the idea that I'm now living in three different places: Japan, where I work; Italy, where my wife's family live; and England, where I was born. Of course, this is a state of mind, rather than a material fact.' Would you like to talk about the impact of this situation on your work, and the ways in which the textures of your poems evoke this as a 'state of mind'?*

**Peter Robinson**: Early printings of 'On Van Gogh's La Crau' have as an epigraph a few lines from Coleridge's poem to his brother George: 'Me from the spot where first I sprang to light / Too soon transplanted, ere my soul had fixed / Its first domestic loves ...' That was putting a local habitation and a name to why I feel a sense of displacement practically all the time. I guess the impact of this situation on my work is just one of the founding facts about it. That's how I perceive the world. That's why there's something to report on – to Jean Kemp, for example, a little friend who I left behind when at the age of three I moved to Liverpool. So the state of mind is like Wordsworth in the Preface to *Lyrical Ballads* when he talks about the poet being peculiarly likely to be affected 'by absent things as if they were present' – to which I could add by present things as if they were absent. I might then be writing to register more forcefully to myself the presence of what is present, and to realize concretely the sensed presence of things absent, and then to accommodate both to each other. So I would imagine that the rhythms and the evocations and the occasioned speech in the poems are aiming at achieving some realization and integration of these disparate materials.

*Would you talk a little about your methods of composition, the occasions of your poems? Have things changed at all over the years?*

My first way of writing poems was to scribble down what I thought were cleverly-turned bitter jokes that caught, or I imagined they did, the contradictions and injustices of the world as I became aware of them in early teenage. Then there was a phase of crude imitation in which I took a model like a Blake song, or a Mauberley quatrain poem, or a bit of Joyce's *Ulysses* and did an over-written version of it. The first poem I wrote which gets anywhere near my vein was about my father's dad, and was compared to a Beatles song by David Moody when I first went up to York in 1971. There I read in my first year Vladimir Mayakovsky's *How are Verses Made? The Waste Land* manuscript was published at about the same time. Then began a three or four year phase of imitating and absorbing and learning how to revise. Still, my only method was to slap down whatever came into my head and then slowly try to get some of the better bits to work as a poem. It was only in my mid to late twenties that I started learning how to listen for what was forming, put it down in a notebook, then slowly let it grow either in my head or on paper and, with luck and patience, both.

*You seem to be quite prolific at the moment?*

Yes, the poems have been coming unusually frequently over the last few years. Mind you, I've never ever worried about where the next one was coming from, and only very occasionally have I had droughts of a month or more. However, there have been times when the number of poems I thought publishable was suddenly very low. I used to have long bad patches. Perhaps I've got better at listening for the right things and letting them come naturally. Maybe the critical faculty is screening out wastes of effort before they even get started. Still, a prolific spell is just the time to grow wary.

*What line, if any, do you take on the notion of a poem being 'abandoned' or 'completed'?*

I don't abandon many poems, because I'm stubborn. When I've completed a poem I'll either decide it's not worth sending out, or send it out a few times, and then decide it's not right; or it will get accepted and then I'll wonder whether that means it's an acceptable poem or not. But I don't go along with the Valéry distinction at all. As far as I'm concerned, 'abandoned' poems aren't finished and shouldn't be published. In other words, I don't make a fetish of perfection.

*You have written about poetry and attempted 'reparation'. Would you like to talk about the relationship between this and revision?*

I've done just that, at length, in my first critical book. There's an analogical relationship between 'revision' and 'reparation'. All of it goes back to the rape I witnessed when I was 'just a kid, maybe twenty-two, / Neither good nor bad, just a kid like you …' If you look at the poem 'There Again' it's all spelled out: writing the poem is seeing again what happened, and seeing again is 'revising', and in poetry 'revising' is, or we hope it is, making things better, and that might be, analogically as I say, performing an emblematic action in order to admit a measure of complicity, which is 'reparation', and so you write and revise in order to make things better. Well, it has to be attempted reparation, because the emblematic action in art can't be assumed to translate into life. The reader and the addressee have to take the measure of what the poem is doing. If they don't want to, there's nothing I can do about it: I'm on my own again. Barbara Everett caught this problem in a recent piece on the new J C C Mays edition of Coleridge's poems when she wrote that the 'process of regret and redress can be carried out by a writer only as an act of communication, of sharing'. So I'm another forever trying to waylay wedding guests.

*Then how do you feel about your reception over the years? Reviewers have found it hard to pigeonhole your work, but they still have a go (such as John Ashbery's re-working of Bloom's 'strong poets' in* PN Review *to list you under the 'curiously strong'). Would you like to give them some guidance for future reference?*

T S Eliot says in his introduction to a choice of Kipling's verse that he's just trying to keep his man out of the wrong pigeonholes. I've taken that to heart and tried to keep out of all pigeonholes. Just to give a symptomatic instance of the problem from a recent, generous and positive review for which I can't and shouldn't complain: there, the reviewer says I'm like Larkin and cites as evidence the single phrase: 'what will survive of us / is things'. But doesn't that mean that I'm veering away – note the pointed line break – from 'An Arundel Tomb' by the sub-stituted noun, and signalling it by the odd grammar of the verb 'to be' with a singular subject and a plural predicate? The same poem ('Not Yet Out of the Wood'), being about an obsessive devotion to writing and how that is impacting on a relationship, is full of allusion to the poets. There's Dante in the title, Auden's Yeats elegy, W S Graham's analogy of snow and writing, a Shakespearean stage direction, and a Giorgio Caproni epigram. The line that's supposed to be pure Larkin is crossed with a bit about his father's 'things' in Vittorio Sereni's 'Il Muro'. And the last line ('do I wait or go?') must be recalling Keats's 'Ode to a Nightingale'. Yes, I'm the sort of poet who likes poetry; and you don't need to 'get' these allusions to understand or enjoy the poem. But, then, if you're referring to allusions in a review? The kind reviewer also noticed that my *Selected Poems* contains an epigraph from Sereni's work and a dedication to him, and has probably noticed too that I've been involved in translations of his and other people's poems and prose. Yet there we are, I'm like Larkin, that poet who famously had no use for foreign poetry. So my advice to future reviewers would be just to try and do a good job: read it properly and then think about the cohesiveness of what you're saying about it.

*Following on from this, many of your poems and essays show a heightened sensitivity regarding the reader or 'addressee' or 'interlocutor'. Would you talk about this, especially in your ability to turn, or change in pitch, modes of address within a poem, forcing the reader to re-appraise initial presumption?*

How addicted we all are to talking about art with the vocabulary of bullying and torture! Am I 'forcing' anybody to do anything? The reader is entirely free to put the book down and not to 're-appraise' at all. If readers are doing that, then they are voluntarily undergoing the experience of allowing their minds and bodies to be moved by these words – which they themselves have to activate for anything to be happening. Sure, I like to put readers through their paces. One reason for this is that I'm the first reader, and in that sense I'm presumably the interlocutor being talked to as well. So I must be inviting myself to re-appraise my initial presumptions too. Another kind of answer to your question, though, would just be to go back to Jean Kemp and say that my poetry wants to talk to people I can't speak to any more: distant relatives, lost friends, people who've died. Or it wants to talk to those I can, my family, for instance – but to talk in ways that are not socially sanctioned, or which make something more emblematic of our words than the endlessly exciting and ephemeral stream of even the best conversation.

*In a recent review of Christopher Reid's* For and After *in the* TLS, *you discussed the balancing act between private dedication and the public domain of readership: 'the danger in poems privately occasioned is that we can't merely be told of the significance in the event of life; we have to be allowed to live it once more with meaning.' Would you talk about the ways in which you deal with such a danger in your own writing?*

By being very sparing with the dedications, for one thing. There are lots of 'unknown' interlocutors. Writing in a now-published private journal from 1989, Dylan Francis referred to my 'self-deprecating subject matter' as 'almost a stalking horse'. The thing is that I don't write about intimate relations of family, love, or friendship because, or only because, of their meaning in my life. After all, there are lots of people close to me to whom I have not dedicated poems, or rendered events of our lives into verse. How does the 'choice' get made? There has to be something that appears humanly and culturally worth exploring, evolving, developing, and perhaps resolving, in a piece of art. There has to be the light bulb going on in my head that says 'maybe there's a poem there'. So I deal with the danger (though I mentioned it in the review because it's been pointed to in poems of mine) by trying to write with the other interlocutors whom I don't know personally in the forefront of my mind. And the way to do that is to concentrate wholly upon what the words of the poem can be understood to mean by anyone who knows the English language and pays a reasonable amount of attention to those words.

*Towards the end of your essay 'Envy, Gratitude and Translation', apropos Matthew Arnold's notion of the 'union of the translator with his original', you come to this conclusion: 'Translation is the correlation of significant differences.' Would you like to talk about your own experiences as translator in the light of this comment?*

I made that comment in the light of my experiences as a translator and as a man loving a woman. I thought Arnold's remark sounded like fantasy sex. In a thoughtful review of the book of mine you published, *The Great Friend and Other Translated Poems*, the reviewer says that 'the skills of the translator, while restructuring the poem in its new language, lie in minimizing the losses'. Then he adds, quoting the blurb: 'if the aim becomes to make "English poems in their own right", something must give.' But I don't see why it must. There can be no union of the original with the translation. So they must be, at best, significantly different. The translator of poetry has to translate the fact that his text is a poem, and has to translate as closely as possible what it means, which, in the case of a poem also includes the occasion for its utterance and such like. I've been collaborating on translations of my own poems into Italian just recently. The texts will face each other. The aim has to be to have produced two poems. If the translation turns out well in its language, then I'm happy. If that requires rephrasing, or altering an idiom, or dropping the rhyme scheme, so be it. One of the things a faithful translator might do, after all, is to try and curb the desire to finesse an arbitrary gain, to out-do the occasion. That's what I meant by correlating the differences: you work on the translation so that it has its own integrity as English, and its integrity as a faithful approach to the original.

*Changing tack only slightly, would you like to qualify or expand upon what a reviewer in the* TLS *called your 'important relationship with Vittorio Sereni'?*

My wife is from Parma, where Vittorio Sereni's eldest daughter and liter-ary executor lived. Those two poems, 'Unfaithful Translations' and 'Towards Levanto', bring together the work of translating Sereni and the process of falling in love, even though I was already married. So the important relationship is with my future second wife, and as far as Sereni is concerned the relationship is strictly with his poetry – which is being alluded to strongly in both those poems of mine. The close of 'Towards Levanto' ('the possible, Vittorio, your sea') links back to 'An Impossibility', dedicated to my now wife, and alludes to the third part of Sereni's 'Un posto di vacanza', which evokes feeling tempted by memories of sexual desire on that same coast. There are moves afoot to publish a large selection of Sereni's poetry and prose with an American university press, so perhaps making those links will become easier for people less familiar with European poetry. I only met Sereni himself twice before his painfully early death at 69. It would have been a pleasure, I think, to get to know him better; but it was not to be.

*When did you start writing, and sending out for publication? Can you describe the motivations or promptings that started things off?*

I started writing with an aim to make art at about the age of sixteen. Almost immediately I started giving things to people who were editing school publications. I submitted a sheaf of verses and won the 'Old Pupil's English Poem' prize at Liverpool College in June 1971. Then I appeared regularly in student magazines at York. I started sending out in about 1975. One of my earliest rejections was from Tim Longville at the *Grosseteste Review.* I had sent some would-be Objectivist lyrics – which I called 'Minimal Poems'. He wrote back a long and kind letter pointing out that they were nothing like 'minimal' enough to count. I hadn't read Cid Corman then. What was my motivation? One morning during my year in the lower sixth (we were studying *A Portrait of the Artist as a Young Man*) I woke up and just punched the pillow with the realization that James Joyce's book about his religion, sexual trouble and Dublin made perfect sense of my religion, sexual trouble and Liverpool. If he could do it, so would I. Doubtless, there have been thousands of young people who've had similar experiences; but, as I say, I'm stubborn and I stuck at it. I remember my A-level art master – he was also the Rugby coach – picking up one of my expressionistic landscapes about then and saying: 'Rob, Rob, what are you trying to prove?' Good question.

*Would you talk a little about editorial policies and your decisions in placing poems with particular poetry magazines and journals? Your poems are to be found in 'shoestring' avant-garde journals such as* Shearsman *or* Tears in the Fence, *and well-heeled places like the* TLS...

My answer would have to be prefaced by the fact that decisions made about where my poems appear have not tended to be made by me! I have a drawer of rejection slips I occasionally open and immediately close again. One of the consequences of trying to keep out of the pigeonholes may be that you don't feel perfectly at home in any magazine. They are all slightly disorientating galleries in which to find things on display. The oddity of my appearing in the very precarious ones and in a News International paper on alternate weeks, as it were, is the result of suddenly being 'taken up' by a few of the main venues at the age of 50. I fear that their interest may well prove a flash in the frying pan. Someone said recently he'd seen another of mine in the *TLS*; and then added that I had clearly perfected the art of the one-inch-deep poem. You're just not likely to see a three-page piece of mine, 'The Relapses' for instance, in that paper. No, it appeared in John Matthias's *Notre Dame Review*, the nearest thing I have to a home in the USA. The shoestring magazines are the places where I started publishing; and the ones I like have friendly editors with distinctive, but still pretty catholic tastes. There are some poets I hear who only allow their work to appear in 'the best' places. I wouldn't like to have that sort of attitude. If practically anybody asks me for something, I tend to send. Living a long way from everywhere, I find it reassuring to keep up contacts with a wide range of publications. Not being able to draw sustenance from the ground any longer, I'm the kind of plant that has had to develop a large number of air roots.

*Could you talk a little about* Perfect Bound *and* Numbers, *two magazines that you helped to edit ...*

One of the first galleries where I thought my work hung rather oddly was *Perfect Bound*. 'Worlds Apart', in the first issue and the first poem in the *Selected Poems*, sounds too personal, provincial, and human – all too human, for that particular zoo. The various issues of the magazine might be seen as an attempt to surround my poems with work that would make it appear less lonely, or simultaneously with attempts to write in ways that would not stick out so much – both impossible, more or less, in the end. We had a rule with *Numbers* that the two editors who were poets wouldn't publish their own work (though we allowed translations). *Numbers* was a bit like that definition of a camel: a horse designed by a committee. We produced some interestingly varied issues; but it was instructive to find that we would endlessly debate whether to publish a couple of poems by an obscure figure from one clique or another, while the big names from those same cliques would get in on the nod. That was upsetting.

*Have there been any defining moments in your career to date, what reviewers like to call 'breakthrough moments'?*

I don't think of myself as having a career as a poet or a writer. For me it's more of an obsession. People go into a career with the idea that it's going to give them a salary. Speaking in those terms, though, a breakthrough moment might be when John Welch of The Many Press agreed to do a collection with a spine in 1979. It might be when Michael Schmidt at Carcanet said he would look at a manuscript in 1985 and eventually accepted it. Then there's the day Martin Dodsworth reviewed that book – *This Other Life* – in *The Guardian* (13 May 1988), a day I walked around in a daze of fondly imagined fulfillment. Or there's the evening he gave the book a little prize in that same year. I've been lucky. There have been lots of them. But in terms of the obsession, well, it's moments like one night and morning in September 1976. I went to bed in Little Venice after just noting down straight the first seven lines of 'Overdrawn Account' as they stand in the *Selected Poems*, and then woke up with the following twenty-one just waiting to be written. That was one of the first poems that 'just came out that way' and I liked it.

*How difficult was it to 'select' for your* Selected? *Was it especially difficult to choose from the early work?*

Not very – I just picked the ones that demanded not to be left out. The early work was the easiest, because there are poems there that strike me as tentative steps down roads not really taken. They can, most of them, go into a *Collected Poems*, all being well, but those pieces complicate the early story with hesitations and I thought they could be spared the dim glare of further publication for now. There were also early poems, 'Some Hope' for instance, where I had wanted to print a revised text almost from the moment that they appeared in the first pamphlets and collection.

*Over the years, since we first met in 1979, what, in the words of your 1997
collection's title, have you 'lost and found'?*

Ah yes, 'The art of losing isn't hard to master', as Elizabeth Bishop has it.
I've lost my first love, and our precariously settled situation in Britain.
We were finally divorced in about 1994. I've lost the hearing in one ear,
from the very invasive surgery required to remove a brain tumour in
1993. I've lost the ability to cry out of my right eye and my broad and bal-
anced smile, for the same reason. I've lost the feeling, or merely
assumption, that my native land is where I ought to be. I've lost illusions
about the literary world and the literary life – but perhaps not all of
them. I've gained my second love, whom I first met in 1984 and married
eleven years later. I've been able to have a family: two daughters. Thanks
to the Japanese education system, I have a job and a salary. Thanks to
many people, including you, I've a reputation, or something like the start
of one, for what I am able write.

Peter Robinson

Five Poems

THERE AGAIN

I

Our witnesses were just visible views,
mountains north-west of Milan,
as lightning flashes at four in the morning
revealed taut power lines,
and by crash barriers, puddled verges
encroached on hard shoulder;
a cloud burst dissolving the distances
softened reddish clay earth –
the predictable returns of windscreen wipers
like mitigating circumstances.

2

Yet seeing the muzzle of an automatic weapon,
(his other hand fumbling
with your tricky brooch) I nearly relive
the taste sour breath has
harsh against your expressionless face,
and the unutterable humbling
my being there couldn't relieve.

3

Driven into a landscape without choices –
where no law was applicable
but his common sense's
wanting an object, you would serve.
And wait was all I had to do.
Because the first thing's to survive,
you said you'd bear the consequences,
whatever he demanded, giving me
occasion to revise or think again
how in that lay-by, and alive,
we viewed each other differently.

UNFAITHFUL TRANSLATIONS

*'e acque ci contemplano e vetrate,*
*ci pensano al futuro: capofitti nel poi,*
*postille sempre più fioche*
*multipli vaghi di noi quali saremo stati.'*
— Vittorio Sereni

In the lake of the Parco Ducale at Parma
dark carp swam beneath the surface
of their spacious liquid; someone
almost too close to me called them
to my trembling, airy attention
and I tried to touch those depths still without harm.

At Segrate, artificial waters between windows
contemplating us would reproduce
intersecting figures in each ripple and glass pane;
I also saw the fat-fed fish
pursuing their own ends, those
ringlets of disturbance which were first signs of rain.

But not enough time, there is never the time
to learn how to say what we mean:
'*Buon lavoro!*' won't translate into 'Good work!'
or 'friendly', *amichevolmente*;
yet well-meant misunderstandings
finally reached me – each faint, part-remembered droplet
of the second and last time we met.

Late perhaps, perhaps distorted, but your words
came offering in trust
– substance, I'm to realise,
a counterbalance to perpetually lost
body, voice, touch, absorbed eyes
as though inviting me towards
myself, a life, the knowledge you have left us.

THE HAPPINESS PLANT

There was a mist on the marshalling yards;
a yucca, the happiness plant,
its top sealed with a red solution,
had forced up arms, like Daphne's, at its sides;
the bathroom window had been somehow broken
as if in a struggle or fit of rage
and a yellowed lace curtain, drawn across it,
tried to make light of the jagged shards.

This perishable matter would stay and rot for years
as if to test belief in the power of his fridge
where everything forever may be preserved,
though somebody's gone off with what was legally hers,
and an end game's pieces stood waiting for the end
on an ironing board with a hole burnt in its cloth:
yet what if the opponent would not understand
that the effort itself had taken all our breath?

Outside, incessant noises from machinery and cars
framed the silence of this lofty room
where dusty book jackets, soft toys, what was
the memory of another, outlive the afternoon.
Here pages of a barely to be finished novel lie
variously in sheafs of a latest draft.
Love's failures are carried on and on in other words
and the writing problems have been talked to death.

Across unemptied ashtrays and the minute pause
between clicks on an answerphone, there rises
the wish to avoid being drawn, just suppose,
into another of so many lost causes,
for there is a mist on the marshalling yards
and though a yucca, the happiness plant,
its top sealed with a red solution,
has forced up arms, like Daphne's, at its sides,
the burden of the air still refuses to lift.

('There Again', 'Unfaithful Translations' and 'The Happiness Plant'
are published in *Selected Poems*, Carcanet, 2003)

LANGUAGES OF WEATHER

For a momentary feeling of changed
idiom in an atmosphere,
I'm listening through static, white noise,
through the chores and challenged
dutiful attempts to be here;
I listen for the sound of a voice
as for a passing, brief sensation
in the languages of weather,
something that might have been sensed by
a relative or someone
at the corner of a street, the sky.

Tired, its pitch contour flattens
as on a cardiac monitor,
flat vowels a perpetual surprise
to somebody muffled in headphones
hearing the intonation patterns
of a voice I barely recognize,
known as it sounds through the bones,
one lost and found then lost again
with a serial forgetfulness,
a mirror, clothes hanger, and pen.

'Speak for yourself,' I hear it say –
like slant light piercing an overcast day.

ALIEN REGISTRATION

'Dr. Robinson, you need to renew
your alienation card...'


Daybreak and even the clouds flake
away at their edges like fish scales,
like rust, like blood on your lenses;
and, for a moment, I'm really not sure
where this particular darkness visible
might be, and you know how it is, an obscure
remorse or worse, something worse
sticks round the memories of words;
and I squirm as between a clock and bed,
porous with daylight, darker shapes
fill out the outline in a vanity mirror
speckled at its edges; and sure enough,
glancing at the photograph,
you notice a face they no longer recognize.

So you know, you don't need to be told
how the frustrations will gather
at stuck traffic signals or a stop-sign,
when queues in official places
leave us all at another loose end...
There'll be little else for it but to take
that gap between sky and unfenced concrete
as a storm cloud comes sloping above me
to shed its droplets on the finest grey
dust you might ever hate to see –
being humbled by this disintegrating day
when any slight change in the weather
is enough to be wondering what in the world
could possibly put it back together?

# Richard Tillinghast

## SNOWFLAKES & A JAZZ WALTZ

You have things to do, but the snow doesn't care.
As contemplation leads you
from window to window, the snow
accompanies you.
Whenever you glance up from the page, there it is –
layered, dense, constant.

It amplifies the volume of space
and gives you a way of telling time.

Eradication of emptiness, a specific against *ennui*,
it works, like truth, on a slant.

Its lightness
responds to gravity
by drift and evasion.
As you drive around town
it slackens and intensifies –
a sideways sizzle of dashes and dots.

While you circle the block, visualising a parking place,
listening on tape to the cymbal-glide
and diminished chords of a jazz waltz
from forty years ago
when you were twenty,
a cash register rings

through the buzz and boozy hum of the Village Vanguard
that Sunday afternoon through cocktail chatter and
cigarette smoke exhaled
by people many of whom must now be dead.
Bill Evans is. Scott LaFaro is –
killed in a car crash
decades ago.

But not you. You drive
through the snow and the morning.
Snow drifts and ticks;

Bill Evans vamps,
and Scott LaFaro's fingers slap against the strings
of his standup bass
in time with the Honda's windshield wipers and
tyres whirring over packed snow.

It snows while you go into the bank and buy euros
and it's snowing when you
come out again.

Snowflakes – white constellations
dissolving.
        Indelible
snowflakes
printing the book of your hours.

## Peter Porter

### WHY DID DANTE PICK ON SUICIDES?

Life is someone's gift: Dante thought it God's.
Doggerel or great verse or what's to hand
Can warm the after-life. The *Afterwards*
Of Hardy morphs full-stop to ampersand.

And this is not great verse – it's written for
Those loved unhappy shades whom Dante turned
To sticks or marl. Forget the every Law
Of Trespass: peace may be strangely earned.

### THE RIDER HAGGARD WINDOW, ST MARY'S, DITCHINGHAM

Time which eats the stories of our lives
Preserves a cruel freshness here to show
How energetic certainty contrives
To tell us what we think we almost know:
The warlike God of England will bestow
At least in retrospect on loyal wives
A school apotheosis, dirge of knives,
With dying, quick in life, in glass made slow.

A dubious transfer this, as history cools,
An ancient trespass, but a change of rules.
The world was opening which today is closed,
And where the mind went destiny would tread
With God and Science noisily opposed
And story-telling garlanding the dead.

**Kate Newmann**

THE ENTRANCE HALL OF ISLA NEGRA
  *for Shay O'Byrne*

A crude spiral of sea-shells
embedded in the circular floor.

Neruda asked that guests enter barefoot,
feel the brute sensibility of sea

massage itself into their earth-bound soles;
that they might heed the swell of cordiality.

So that before sipping his singular cocktail,
a smudge of foreign newsprint still on his fingers,

donning a beret or panama
from the walk-in wardrobe,

(ponchos hanging self-consciously
beside his Nobel tuxedo, worn once),

before enduring the land-locked chatter
under the mural of lapis, onyx and quartz,

he would have them remember ball – arch – callous,
the thinness of permeable skin.

## Katherine Duffy

HAUTE COUTURE

On Howth Head,
the sky is my big blue hat,
still bright around the rim
although the world begins
to dress down for evening.

An early moon's a jewel
in the navel of a muddy puddle;
birds fly low, mocking a distant jet
with their easy, unfuelled, aeroplane chic.

Old's the new new, I'm told,
so my hat's the latest thing
attached to my shoulders by tall,
avant-garde, invisible poles.

The promontory itself gives me height
more striking than any platform shoe.
I wobble slightly, with the joy of walking here;
my hat quivers imperceptibly.

Tony Curtis

ANOTHER ROOM

This was our room,
it has four walls,
I counted them
when you left:

The one with the door,
the one with our pictures,
the one with the window,
the one with our bed.

But now, to put away the memory
of how your hands, your mouth
turned my skin into electricity,
I have taken myself away.

I have moved to another room.
It too has four walls,
but the door opens to the other side,
and there are no pictures of you.

And in the dark,
when I bury your ghost,
the memory of your touch
goes out with the light.


– from *What Darkness Covers*, published in 2003 by Arc Publications.

# Ron Houchin

## PLAYING IN THE CEMETERY

There's a game between moon
and trees. Through whole
winters, elms and maples reach for
the light, and it is magnified by their fingers.

They hold it up pretending it can spin.
For hours they let it believe
there's no such thing as sun.
Each time the wind pulls a cloud tarp

from the playing field, the match is
on then between blue light
and long limbs. Together they point
to the frailest names on tombstones:

*P*'s worn to backward *c*'s and all
the dates losing time. I understand
the changing players, some of the rules,
but how does anything above ground win?

**Ron Houchin**

HEART SHAPE

Out of the dark centre of February,
birds wake remembering the river,
a pink hint of false dawn fevering the surface.
Dogs trot, three following one, in early
glow. Worn leaves wear further in near-morning
wind. They tumble along close to the road,
and at hedges stop. Small sparrows running
with them skitter on to road's edge, pecking
tiny stones, and fluttering back into
the half-light of dream...

My dream, I guess, for I wake looking out
the window beside you. Balsam trees shake
darkness from their hair. And your slow breaths come
beneath shadows of limbs. Where are you now?
I trace the heart shape of your breasts, and lips
that puff slightly. The last of night is
antique. I reach beneath the covers for your
other heart shape. My tongue finds the cleft.

# Dennis O'Driscoll

Clare Brown and Don Paterson (editors), *Don't Ask Me What I Mean: Poets in Their Own Words*, Picador, 2003, £16.99.

A party at which all the guests are poets – and all the poets are gabbing non-stop about their own work – might not be everybody's mug of mead. One imagines the bouncers being kept busy separating squabbling bards rather than ejecting groupies and gatecrashers found lurking suspiciously behind the laurel hedge. *Don't Ask Me What I Mean* is a party thrown by the Poetry Book Society in London for its golden anniversary; and a very civilised occasion it actually proves to be, consisting of short sharp self-observations contributed to the *Poetry Book Society Bulletin* over the past half-century. The quarterly *Bulletin*, issued to members of this heroic organisation which battles tirelessly and thanklessly for contemporary poetry, allows poets whose new collections are awarded the 'much-coveted' Choice or the 'bittersweet consolation' of a Recommendation by the Society's selectors a platform from which to introduce and discuss their work.

In the Poetry Book Society, many are called but few are chosen. Although most publishers submit typescripts of forthcoming poetry collections, only one volume per quarter is accorded 'Choice' status and issued to members. The print-run of the chosen collection will be instantly boosted (turbo-charged in proportion to normal poetry sales) by about 2,000 copies. There are over 300 pages of mini-essays in *Don't Ask Me What I Mean*; while these are drawn from British and Irish poets in the main, the invitation list – assembled by the poet Don Paterson (who excludes his own spirited contributions to past *Bulletins*) and Clare Brown (who recently retired as Director of the Poetry Book Society) – also extends to some familiar figures from America, the antipodes and elsewhere.

The book makes for a surprisingly lively shindig; the quality of the contributions is generally high and the company – whether of the fashionable, the firm or the fast-fading – is often congenial. For sure, there are times when the arrogance, triumphalism and presumption on display become as nauseating and stomach-churning as a pint of beer slops or a curdled canapé; and someone's insistence that all his dead ducks are wild swans at Coole may tempt you to mumble your excuses and slam the book shut like a door. But you will be in no hurry whatsoever to leave if you find yourself positioned in the more commodious corners of the room where wiser counsel – that of Philip Larkin and James Reeves, say – prevails. Ted Hughes is nearby, offering seminal insights into his poems ('they are the only way I can unburden myself of that excess which, for their part, bulls in June bellow away') and he presents a convincing portrait of a poetically possessed Sylvia Plath in the eye of the creative whirlwind that became *Ariel* ('These are poems written for the most part at great speed, as she might take dictation…The words in these odd-looking verses are not only charged with terrific heat, pressure and clairvoyant precision, they are all deeply related within any poem, acknowledging each other and calling to each other in deep harmonic designs'). As well as Ted Hughes, other poets of the recent past who make memorable contributions to *Don't Ask Me What I Mean* include R S Thomas, Kathleen Raine and Charles Causley, their engaging voices complementing – and sometimes conflicting with – those of widely-read contemporaries as various as Ian Duhig and Helen Dunmore, Michael Longley and Michael Hofmann, Geoffrey Hill and U A Fanthorpe.

It may be plausibly argued that these commentaries by poets are – in the absence of their poems – mere liner notes without the recording, a glossy menu without the sizzling main course. But many of the essays conjure their own music (Eavan Boland's, in which she modulates her sentences like lines of verse, is among the most lyrical) and are substantial and satisfying repasts in themselves (C K Williams dishes up an entire feast of ideas). In slicker instances, the poets behave like estate agents: ushering the reader around a collection, pointing out its special features (a nice pair of matching rhymes here, smoothly sanded stanzas there, oodles of storage space everywhere), while their suave palaver diverts attention from the leaks, cracks and creaks. Other poets are more subtle, simply hinting at the imaginative investment potential on offer for the shrewd reader and the book's capacity – subject, no doubt, to planning permission – to expand the mind.

The sensible, solidly-crafted structure is the one most favoured by the Poetry Book Society selectors; ultra-Modernist experimenters (the *ampersandeurs* as the editors caricature them) are as sparse as Brutalist architects at a Prince of Wales ball. As for 'location, location, location', Charles Causley (dependable and unostentatious as a gable wall) and Norman Nicholson (his jolly face half-timbered by extravagant sideburns) were like listed cottages in the small English towns that gave them poetic sustenance. To TS Eliot's line, 'Home is where one starts from', Nicholson – a lifelong lodger in the Cumbrian house where he was born – ruefully yet proudly adds a personal gloss: 'It seems to be where I finish.' Train journeys have driven Sean O'Brien to some of the best poems of his generation. A jaunt through the Holy Land in a clapped-out Mercedes jolted Simon Armitage's collection *The Dead Sea Poems* into motion. Douglas

Dunn, having captured *Terry Street* – the Hull slum which he placed permanently on the poetry map – downplays the value of location: 'The only way I can try to describe the poetry I have written so far, and it is not really for me to do this, is to suggest that I have tried to understand the familiar and the ordinary, and that locality has little to do with this.'

Reading the testimonies of poets, as they emerge dazed or dazzled from the darkroom of composition, one is confirmed in the view that even the fullest disclosure in prose – however fascinating – can never adequately account for the poetic act it describes. Although George Barker was a notorious windbag, he neatly summarises the impossibility of writing conclusively about one's own creations: 'If I could put into five hundred words what these poems are about I would certainly not have wasted my time and paper elaborating those five hundred words into a lot of verses.' Better still is R S Thomas's analogy with dance: 'I am chary about writing about my poetry at all. I still remember Anna Pavlova's answer to the question as to what her dance meant: "If I could tell you in words, do you think I would go to the immense trouble of dancing it?"' It is the conscious, effortful parts of writing – the deskwork of editing, redrafting, revising, rather than the headwork conducted by the subconscious – that can be most readily and accurately charted. The poetic process itself is ferociously difficult to analyse without immediately striking the rocks of mystification and obfuscation. On the one hand, even after years of practice, a poet is every bit as likely to 'fail again' worse as better ('past performance is no guarantee of future results', as the investment ads remind us). On the other hand, if the poet is exceptionally fortunate, the poem of a lifetime may be written when all the necessary elements – emotional, technical, rhythmical and verbal – coincide as miraculously and marvellously as a blue moon and a midnight sun. Far from being regularly showered with profligate kisses by the Muse, many poets – at one time full of thrusting promise and eager expectation – experience the same letdown as Dylan Thomas's *Under Milk Wood* character, Bessie Bighead: 'Gomer Owen...kissed her once by the pig-sty when she wasn't looking and never kissed her again although she was looking all the time.'

In poetry, as in taxation, self-assessment can lead to misdeclarations. Poets who act as their own critics may make too many allowances for themselves and seek unearned praise; or they may underdeclare their achievement by affecting an overly modest pose. Vernon Scannell identifies the twin dangers faced by poets filing their *Poetry Book Society Bulletin* returns: either 'seeming absurdly pompous and self-aggrandising' or 'sounding a note, no less offensive, of facetious and phoney self-disparagement'. It is very much to the credit of the contributors to *Don't Ask Me What I Mean* that genuine, credible self-disparagement is frequently encountered. To many serious poets, so great is the gap between aspiration and achievement that a healthy sense of failure, rather than delusions of poetic grandeur, is what drives them onwards. One is happy for Mark Doty, who is 'stunned – and deeply gratified – by readers' responses', yet mighty relieved to find in Anthony Hecht a reflective poet for whom 'There is a way in which a poet's work is for him always a failure and a disappointment, since he alone once entertained the vision of what it might supremely be'. Soaring self-esteem is the least of Thom Gunn's faults as he introduces his collection, *Touch*: 'I find the book difficult to speak about. I sent it off confidently, but by the time I got the proofs a certain revulsion had set in, and my main feeling by now is that, after six years, it doesn't really add up to very much.' I feared that Wendy Cope had gone to self-deprecatory extremes when she seemed to be admitting that her latest collection contains a poem she absolutely loathes: 'There are...three poems about paintings – two poems I quite like and one I dislike intensely.' Having checked the original source (a scholarly euphemism for my dusty rummage through back issues of the *Poetry Book Society Bulletin*), I discovered that it was one of the paintings – not the poems – that had drawn Cope's ire; what she actually wrote referred to 'two paintings I quite like and one I dislike intensely'. Further misprints to puzzle readers of the sometimes aptly-named *Don't Ask Me What I Mean* include references to an apparently talent-spotting London publisher called Seekers and to a hitherto unknown Seamus Heaney poem titled 'Borland', adrift presumably in Ulster between the bog and the border.

There are poets in this book who emphasise the importance of metaphor and mystery, of the oral and aural, of form and flow. But isolating the atomic components of a poem can provide only the vaguest notion of how these parts bond and unite to form a definitive poetic whole. Like the 'dark matter' swirling around the universe, the creative energy which fuses a true poem together can more readily be inferred than formulated. Where this excellent and enjoyable book is at its best is not as a 'how I did it' – let alone a 'how to do it' – manual, but as a source of the kinds of enlightenment that a good poetry reading may yield: down-to-earth annotation, honest-to-God clarification, anecdotes that are windows of illumination.

'There's not much point in talking on a dead line', Charles Causley – pondering the desired ratio of simplification to suggestibility in a poem – declared. *Don't Ask Me What I Mean* helps to eliminate the static in many lines of poetry and to improve the level of communication and understanding between the writer and the reader. And so the conversation at this poetry party goes on, with nearly everyone managing to make themselves as clear as the dawn that is starting to crack open outside the venue.

The amber dewdrops in the lawn below the drawing-room window are mimicking the early sunlight. Feeling a little tired, yet more than a little inspired, the partying poets want to head back quickly to their desks in the hope of drafting a morning-after aubade. Patting their pockets for the car keys, each in turn is urging the Muse – the Poetry Book Society's perpetual guest of honour – to accept a lift and accompany them home.

# Austin Clarke

## OLD-FASHIONED PILGRIMAGE

The following essay, dating from 1967, is published in *Don't Ask Me What I Mean: Poets in Their Own Words*, and is reproduced here with kind permission of Dardis Clarke, 17 Oscar Square, Dublin 8.

I cannot claim to have seen Queen Victoria on her last visit to Ireland, owing to lack of interest. My father lifted me up in the middle of the Dublin crowd but my attention was held by the decorations at the city boundaries.

I had not even heard of the Irish literary revival or the Abbey Theatre till my first year as an undergraduate. I was fortunate, therefore, in catching a last glimpse of an exciting period and in meeting Yeats, Æ, Lady Gregory and others. When my first poem was published in a local periodical, a friend brought me to one of Æ's literary gatherings on a Sunday evening. Æ said a few encouraging words and made me sit beside him. I was bewildered to find that everyone was discussing politics. Suddenly the poet turned and introduced me to a queer-looking little man on my left. This was James Stephens, and I was delighted for I had been reading his *Hill of Vision*. He glanced up at me sharply and said, 'That was very good verse of yours but I hope you don't think it was poetry.' Undaunted by this reproof, I came again on the following Sunday. On my way home, I found myself in the tram beside James Stephens. This was too much for me and I did not return to Æ's house until several years later, when I had written my first book. I had learned my lesson and realised how firmly the poetic privileges and rules were guarded.

I saw most of the early plays of Yeats at the Abbey Theatre and, when the curtain fell, the author appeared outside it, a dim figure against the footlights. He was still the Poet of the Celtic Twilight, swaying, waving his arms rhythmically, telling us in a chanting voice about his 'little play'. I was determined to write verse plays, despite the fact that small size of the Abbey audience on these occasions indicated that it was not a popular pursuit. Eventually I sent a verse comedy to Yeats, asking respectfully for advice. It came back after six months with a badly typed note, in which the poet quoted a few lines in very free rhythm to show that I 'should have written the play in prose'. When I settled down in London in the early twenties, I met George Moore, whose later Greek and Irish romances I admired very much. He, too, was a strict Victorian. One evening, after dinner, he read out a lyric of mine which he liked.

When he came to the second stanza, he stopped and said severely, 'There are two syllables missing in the first two lines.' I pointed out that I wanted to suggest the effect of an otter suddenly diving. 'No, no,' exclaimed Moore, 'the lines in every stanza should match.' The master of the most subtle rhythm in modern prose would permit no liberty to verse! Today young poets can do what they wish and need not feel that they are committed to any particular movement.

Few critics realise how powerful was the influence of the Irish literary movement. This was due not only to the rediscovery of Gaelic mythology and poetry, but also to the fact that it was one of the last phases of the great Romantic Movement. I found myself writing long poems about our heroic period without knowing very clearly why I was doing so. I climbed into upper glens to find the right setting for them. Once, however, on a sunny morning, I trespassed into the Seven Woods at Coole, where Yeats and Æ

> Have seen immortal, mild, proud shadows walk.

Suddenly I saw a rich blue gleam dart through the distant leaves. Was I to see a vision too? A moment later I saw the blue flash again. Wondering if it were a peacock, I crept closer and peeped between the branches. Crossing a lawn towards a Georgian mansion, I saw a tall fisherman wearing a raincoat of sky-blue watered silk. To my astonishment, I recognised Yeats. He had become the ideal Fisherman of the poem he was to write many years later.

Despite my sceptical temperament, I found it difficult to avoid the visional intensity of my elders, especially when the temptation towards superstition took the form of woman. Ella Young, pale, ethereal, dressed in grey flowing silks, looked like an ancient priestess, and when she lit a joss stick and spoke of ancient gods, I found it hard to resist. Maud Gonne was as fascinating when she spoke of her awareness of the Invisible Land. She had drawn Yeats into revolutionary politics but he had lured her even farther into the visionary past. It was not until 1928, when I published Night and Morning, that I found myself back in the present.

The title poem of Old-Fashioned Pilgrimage is a description of a visit I paid to America to see places associated with writers whom I read when I was adolescent: Emerson and Thoreau had had much influence in the early days of the Irish revival. Professor Edward Dowden was one of the first to praise Whitman, and TW Rolleston translated Leaves of Grass into German. Among other subjects dealt with in the book are Vietnam, the Pill and Ecumenism, grave and gay.

Macdara Woods

Balancing Above Niagara

Richard Kell, *Collected Poems 1962–1993*, Lagan Press, 2001, £7.95.
Francis Harvey, *Making Space: New and Selected Poems*, Dedalus Press,
2001, €17.72/€10.10.

Back in the fifties, when I was at school, I was much taken by Pound's
'Ode Pour l'election de son Sepulchre':

> For three years, out of key with his time,
> He strove to resuscitate the dead art
> Of poetry; to maintain "the sublime"
> In the old sense. Wrong from the start...

a poem as layered with meaning for me as the three *Matrix* films are for
any contemporary young aficionado. Did Pound consider the three years
as wasted time? The dead art? Maintain? Sublime? And if three years out
of key with one's time is a bad (though perhaps quasi-heroic) place to be,
then what of a lifetime, twenty, thirty, forty years or more?

A lifetime later, fifty apparently out of key years later, I know that the
hallmark of *l'air du temps* is that no one can say what it is – at the time;
and that nothing dates as sadly as the fashionable, the trendily accessible,
or the assumed, deployed persona that a writer, or the public, has come
to believe in. Coming inevitably to terms with one's own eccentricities is,
of course, another matter.

Both of the writers under review here have given a lifetime to poetry,
with – I hope – more poems to come; both are from Ulster, both in their
seventies, each of them writes out of a recognisable Irish provenance,
both believe in diversity, and neither has received due recognition. The
note on Kell's book describes him as one of Ireland's 'most...unjustly
neglected poets'; the sad truth is that all neglect of the kind suggested is
unjust, and, if you move off the tracks, more usual than not.

The adulatory recognition that does attend a certain few writers is
not mostly to do with the work at all, but comes from a media-related
chimera of perception, or presentation, of publicity or promotion,
whether or not consciously wrought. A fusion of advertising and art, the
beginnings of which were identified – tentatively – by Louis MacNeice in
his play *One For The Grave*, even before the post nineteen sixties pop-deluge
had kicked-in. If I spend time on this it is because reading both of these
poets – Kell in particular – sets up a dialogue, a debate, inside me at any

rate, as to the nature of poetry itself, what it is, where it comes from, and why – even whether – a person should spend their life at it; but I do not know that this dialogue, once set up, is the one he would wish. Nor am I sure in every instance what his own dialogue with himself is about, although it is always clear that there is an argument – an honourable intellectual engagement – going on. It seems to start from an absent place, of incidentals rather than imperatives, as far away from us now, as flickering as Carol Reed's 1947 *mise en scène* in *Odd Man Out*.

Two quotes from Kell's preface may clarify what I mean. In one he describes his Irish roots, North and South, as Protestant and 'British', speaks of 'Methody' Methodist College in Belfast, Wesley and TCD in Dublin, and mentions among his contemporaries during his undergraduate years, Robert Greacen, Sam Harrison, Billy O'Sullivan and Ben Howard, as well as the Glasgow-born Dublin poet Pearse Hutchinson. And, looking back to childhood and upbringing, he also refers approvingly to such proverbial folk-wisdom as 'you're not the only pebble on the beach', 'it's no use crying over spilt milk', and 'look before you leap'. As he admits, these are expressions of petit-bourgeois prudence, but the question is how do they affect him as he engages with poetry.

Fred Johnston's Introduction is instructive, but as can happen with a labour of love, sometimes over-defensive. He draws proper attention to Kell's discipline, the constant experiment with verse forms, his back-rhyming, his fascination with the techniques of writing poetry, to the humanist variety of interests and volume of humane expression. And yet I think he misses the essential humane aspect of Kell's work: that in the progression to knowledge, through age and violent loss and awareness, the petit-bourgeois perspective and sensibility become somehow, at the same time, both overturned and vindicated – become celebratory even, in a poem like 'A Reunion', which is genuinely erotic, but much more than that has an achieved tenderness and vulnerability about it; not so much to do with sex, though it is sexual too, real middle-aged extra-marital sex at that, as with intimacy, an all embracing intimate understanding:

> Meanwhile, what better way
> to pass the uncontracted hours than lie
>   peacefully side by side,
> to drowse, to talk, or, pillow-propped, to read
>   aloud or watch the box.
> Those free-flowing conversations! – childhood, sex,
>   music, the mystery cults,
> political trend, and trendy architects...

A clear thread running through the book is exactly that: the triumph of intimacy, and that we can be redeemed by it.

Sometimes Kell remains preoccupied with the cerebral why, even to the telling extent, in 'Ode in Memory of Jean François Gravelet, called Blondin', of posing sixty-two lines of supposition and query to the high-wire performer doing his balancing act above Niagara Falls ('Niagara has nothing to match your skill: / that huge splayed energy is inept as fat / beside the strength whose terse and accurate jets / could thread the eyes of needles.'); but what of the parallel subliminal anti-message that I see poking out subversively from behind the poem: not to think too much about it, just to keep to the craft and do it? Like the current neo-pragmatic advertisement all over New York: I do therefore I am.

Francis Harvey, on the other hand, can see all in the ruins of a man, as in his marvellous nine line poem 'Viewing the Ruins', which ends...

> The child that he was is the ghost beginning
> to haunt the ruins he thinks is a man.
>
> I watch the old growing old by watching myself.

... a man becoming one with time and place, and more at one perhaps with someone else, momentarily, somewhere-nowhere along the swaying wire from here to there.

If Kell seems to speak almost as the singular amateur, Harvey appears as the Shepherd of the Rocks, and rocks is the word. He has a multitude of ways of talking about stone. He is stone-mad and he knows it:

> What I'm gone in the head about is stone

and there clearly must be a significance to this for Irish artists. It is the same consuming, informed passion shared by the sculptor Seamus Murphy and the painter Tony O'Malley. The Argentine writer Jorge Fondebrider once told me that among his enthusiastically beef-eating fellow-country-men chickens were regarded practically as vegetables; in Harvey's archetypal landscapes even the whin bushes, the hollow rib cages that were dead sheep, as well as the wind that blows through them, take on the quality of stone, that insistent granite silence:

> The silence of the glen is
> the silence at the bottom
> of the sea; he has been drowning in it

for as long as he can remember:
a slow death.

– from 'Condy at Eighty'

Until, in the marvellous new poems, in 'Hail and Farewell' for example, stone has entered into the human body itself, almost as a point of reference, for the compass, the elements, or the Four Last Things:

...and me listening to him
grinding out the last sound he'd ever make
in this world from the depths of his throat like stones
scraping the keel as Charon launched his boat.

In a sense he doesn't stray out of his own discovered landscape, but that's ok, neither did Blake. If you can live in, occupy, space and time as Harvey does, then one body is enough for one history to be all history, one quirk to be all diversity, if we scan it as Harvey does, fully. His is an inhabited *dinnseanchas*, a topography of the spirit, to the extent of being able to describe 'A Place' – a paradigm for all places – by what it is not, the whole plethora of things it is not, peeling away the expected as the wind does, down to bare, acknowledged truth: a place 'beyond all knowing and telling', yet 'with as much claim to being '

as Errigal, Glenveagh or Slieve League,
an empty desolate nameless space dense
with ordinariness and deity.

– from 'A Place'

Or consider the terrifying lines from 'Sheepmen', in the 1996 *Boa Island Janus* collection: Owen McSharry of Crieve, 'on his rack', waiting for the priest to come creaking up the stairs with the Eucharistic 'body of Christ in a box':

A sheepman like himself and the only one
he'd trust to rid him of this thing stuck
like a whinbush in the gap of his throat.

John McAuliffe

IN SEARCH OF THE SECOND LIFE

Tony Lopez, *False Memory*, Salt, 2003, £8.95.
Ian Duhig, *The Lammas Hireling,* Picador, 2003, £7.99.
Don Paterson, *Landing Light*, Faber, 2003, hb £12.99.
Julia Copus, *In Defence of Adultery*, Bloodaxe, 2003, £7.95.
Lavinia Greenlaw, *Minsk*, Faber, 2003, hb £12.99.

British art makes headlines once a year, when the Turner Prize shortlist
'shocks' its audience. For British writers, a similarly antagonistic relation
to their audience is often apparent, although the desire to shock is based
on class and language, rather than subject and form. For writers, this
stance dates perhaps from when John Osborne's Jimmy Porter stuck it
up to his military middle-class in-laws (and by extension, his audience).
The problem is that now (and maybe even then) the audience is already
comfortably on the writers' side, and the oppositional stance only cramps
the poem's possibilities. In spite of this, accent and attitude (framed still
in the traditional forms of Philip Larkin's lyrics) have continued to define
the contemporary British poem. It is a relief then that each of the collec-
tions under review manifests, to different extents, a desire to rework that
paradigm, to either open up the lyric to less predictable kinds of
speaking or to challenge Larkin's formal hegemony.

The latter, more obviously radical approach is proposed by the new
editors of the UK's best-selling periodical *Poetry Review* who have attempted
to shake up and transform their audience's idea of what a poem is. The
new-look journal has provided a platform for various off-shoots of J H
Prynne's linguistically innovative poetry, and has already succeeded in
creating an entirely different picture of the poetry year to that which has
been advanced by the three major poetry prizes, the Forward, Whitbread
and T S Eliot Awards. The latest issue features a number of poems by
Tony Lopez whose *False Memory* offers an accessible entry point to the
kind of new poetry being advanced.

Lopez has composed ten 10-sonnet sequences which quote different
kinds of language and cleverly juxtapose them with one another. The
reader constantly opens a familiar-looking door only to discover another
door behind it that also turns out to look a little familiar, and so on.
Eventually the reader emerges from what feels like an unguided tour of
New Labour Britain and its many jargons. Like some of Paul Muldoon's
recent work, it mixes together private and public phrases to create a
weirdly unfamiliar world. The first poem begins:

And I don't see how we can win. The first faint
Intermittent soundings of the sirens may be ignored
Just as the slogans come through unpractised speech.
In Arcadia, when I was there, I did not see hammering stone
But you should vacate the building when you hear
A continuous note. It is best to move away –
Best to pay bills by direct debit and avoid offices.
Water bombs, I hear, are great fun and completely harmless.

It is interesting and enjoyable work, and no page is without unsettling irony. Its problem is summed up by a disparagement of Larkin, fellow chronicler of England and its idioms, whose 'The Whitsun Weddings' becomes 'An uncle running up to bowl / Someone sampling smut'. Likewise, a backslapping index which functions as a kind of acknowledgments page does nothing for the poems other than remind readers that they are not its intended audience, and that this is art which – in spite of its adherence to the most memorable of short lyric forms – does not identify with the idea that the lyric *can* transcendentally address its reader. Eugenio Montale's 1949 essay, 'The Second Life of Art', discusses how the reader of experimental poetry finds that

> the author has not chosen for him, has not willed something for him,
> he has limited himself to providing a possibility for poetry. This is a
> great deal in itself, but not enough to stay with us after reading. An art
> which destroys form while claiming to refine it denies itself its second
> and larger life: the life of memory and everyday circulation.

The extra challenge of poetry, of imagining meanings, of making, of risking statement, of choosing ways to beat the material into forms that will stick, is – for all the pleasures of these sonnets' witty juxtapositions, satirical allusions and angry, indicting quotation of social attitudes – not an issue for work like Lopez's. However Lopez does, at least, try out alternatives to the modes predominantly chosen by British poets, even though *False Memory* does not seem to imagine for itself the second life described by Montale.

The most prize-nominated book of the past year is Ian Duhig's *The Lammas Hireling* and it is also an interesting collection, and typical of much British poetry in its seemingly oppositional idea about its audience. Duhig likes to confound readers' expectations of poetic gentility: he determinedly refuses lyrical piety and – like his Romantic forbears – often returns poetry to its 'folk' forms; he also introduces and rejects the claims of academic reason, inventing lines of 'research' that lead nowhere outside the poem's ambit; he uses Longley-style litany, but the effect is either sinister or broadly comic; he uses hyperbole dramatically, as in 'Golden Lotus', which viciously gives voice to the muse of a lyric poet:

> Our golden poet thinks my cunt is tight
>
> Because of how the golden lotus makes us walk.
> I haven't walked a step in fifteen years.
> Sometimes he eats almonds from between my toes.
> Sometimes he fucks the cleft in my left foot.

Alongside the satirical redaction of poetic strategies, Duhig plants more straightforward lyrics like 'Midnight on the Water' and fabulous mysteries like the title poem. 'The Lammas Hireling' differs from many other poems here in its sustained ambiguity and sense of (strange) reality: an enjoyable poem like 'Lotus Root Porridge' does not quite take off in the same way and seems content to relish its juxtaposition of delicious phrases. Like Lopez, the surprise of the poem is all in the detail rather than in its overarching formal effect.

Each of Don Paterson's collections has been pre-occupied with re-framing his relationship to the reader. His poems often imagine the spaces in which the poem will be read, most obviously here in 'A Talking Book' which begins in a bookshop, and includes a toilet, a train, a plane and a lift as possible locations for its readings. This is funny although sometimes it seems to be the entire point of the poem that the poem *knows* about you, its reader. It is also an extended riff on the theme of Rilke's 'Archaic Torso of Apollo', a poem translated elsewhere in the collection (and the first evidence of a projected book of Rilke translations to match his versions of Machado in the excellent *The Eyes*). When Paterson (or rather, his 'Talking Book') addresses critics and reviewers he writes:

> ...and a big hi! to those holders, old and new
> of the critic's one day travel pass (I too
> have known that sudden quickening of the pulse
> when something looks a bit like something else...)

which might almost stop his reviewers from mentioning a lot of Northern Irish poets.

The most obvious presence in the collection, though, is the first Paterson style, in the tight, ambivalent short poems set in bed like ''96', 'A Gift', 'One Night' and 'The Wreck' (and a first cousin of this poem, the beguiling Scots 'Twinflooer'). There are also short narratives about journeys that easily take on ambiguous or allegorical meanings, there are a couple of more urban myths and a poem about drinking ('The Shut-In', which shows Paterson's gift for taking an anecdote and freighting it with deeper resonance). Other long poems stray into the realm of the folk and fairy tale as they work out ideas about love, death and art. In some of the narratives, the language is less tense: like Duhig, Paterson easily adopts a cod-academic, reference-quoting speaking voice, but the juxtaposition of this style with an unlikely subject is predictable and unconvincing: '...one other frivolity / refined by Aquinas, tuned up by Bruno / and perfected by Hannibal Lecter', ('The Reading'). In 'My Love', the whole poem reads as if it has been assembled from gingerly handled quotations, from the false logic of 'love is the lover's coin, a coin of no country, / hence: the ring; hence: the moon', to another unlikely authority: 'All of which / brings us to Camille Flammarion, / signing the flyleaf of his *Terres du Ciel*'. Poems like this drift – albeit densely – into a more expansive style, which may not fully work in *Landing Light* (except in the tales 'The Long Story' and 'The Hunt', which seems to be about a Tolkien-like video game), but they do encouragingly suggest that Paterson is not going to simply repeat himself but will continue to try out new ideas and forms as his career progresses.

The interim nature of this collection is best caught in his version of Dante, 'The Forest of the Suicides', where he chooses to use quatrains rather than terza rima. It is studded, characteristically, with concentratedly violent and effective images ('...its human face all wrong / above its fledged gut, wide-winged, razor-clawed'; and 'In the trunk, a red mouth opened like a cut'; and 'naked and still, each hung like a white coat / on the hook of its own alienated shade'); but, like the other long poems here, the poem is also puffed out with the ballad-y likes of 'abysmal need', 'her sullen arts', 'dark trade' and 'mere decency' which do little other than fill in the extra iambic feet till the end of the line. More successful and more 'willed' (to use Montale's term) is the beautiful sonnet, 'Waking with Russell', set –again – in bed, but addressed to his young son, which begins: 'Whatever the difference is, it all began / the day we woke up face-to-face like lovers' and ends 'How fine, I thought, this waking amongst men! / I kissed your mouth and pledged myself forever.'

Julia Copus's *In Defence of Adultery* draws on the kind of alert lyric toughness and variety that Carol Ann Duffy made familiar in *Mean Time*. It is packed with strikingly wry and true lines, like the ending of the title poem, which caps its various definitions of love with: 'Sometimes we manage / to convince ourselves of that'; and the break-up curse of 'Esprit de l'Escalier' which imagines:

> ...the words that I'll throw at you,
> stomping their way up the steps of your heart,

slamming the door shut and settling there, growing
harder, ounce by ounce, like wet cement.

There are entirely successful poems like 'Portrait of My Neighbour
Skipping', 'A Short History of Desire' and the sequence 'Playing It By
Ear' which surprises with its delicate use of the vocabularies of sound
engineering. Copus is the most conventional of the poets under review,
but here she utilises a wider range of material even as the poems shrink
the language to the confining personal relationships at the heart of the
collection's other lyrics, as in 'Conversation at One Metre (60 db)', where

and they talked of the weather,          perhaps, or the imminent
boom in the markets,                      the price of oil,
how it rose or fell,                      according to this or to that.

And of course at the time                neither one of them had
the haziest notion                       of other discussions
they'd hold with that distance           between them – aloof,
or indignant, exhausted,                 despondent.

Lavinia Greenlaw's first two books exercised an impressive control
over their subjects: short sentences, monosyllabic diction, and obscure
and precise detail made for taut, tense poems. She engaged with science,
or the history of science, to provide new material, or new ways of
making connections with an audience. Her great skill was to create an
immediate atmosphere and tone from information, because of how she
set it up at a slightly skewed angle. In *Minsk* Greenlaw risks more of
herself: the unstated pressures suggested in the earlier collections are a
source for reflective comment here, though this does not make the
poems less mysterious or atmospheric, as at the close of the opening
poem, 'The Spirit of the Staircase':

It had been the simplest exchange,
one I'd give much to return to:
the greetings of shadows unsurprised
at having met beneath the trees
and happy to set off again, alone,
back into the dark.

The second poem, 'The Falling City', is typically ambiguous and seems
to start off from a childhood accident. Its obscure angle on the incident is
typical of her earlier work, but the introduction of a more abstract

vocabulary, of forgiveness and love (via a lovely enjambment), typifies Greenlaw's innovations in *Minsk*:

> The world was locked and clear.

> For a moment the glass forgave me,
> curved like a hand that absolutely
> loved me, let me down so gently.

The poems are pained, crystalline, deeply felt and consistently interesting and puzzling. They read like concentrations of effort and skill, craft and an imaginative technique which zeroes in on its subject, ordering it and willing it into particular meanings. The sequence 'A Strange Barn' relates her continuing interest in science to something more than anecdote: in this case, it links the unlikely developments of London Zoo to scientific advances and to cultural changes and cultural resistance to change. The closing sequence, 'The Land of Giving In', does not itself give in to what she might be expected to do with her material: in 'The Boat Back into the Dark', her metaphor insists on difference and change rather than say-ing the same thing again: 'The captain turns the radio on. / 'The Green, Green Grass of Home'. / I try not to sing along.'; while 'The tinsheet-flashlight dramatics of a storm / at three a.m.', which Greenlaw observed in 'Calibration' in her previous collection, has been replaced by the charged, active imagination of 'Bird Walk': 'At three a.m., a black cormorant dives. / A needle, a nightfall, it closes my eyes.' *Minsk* is a collection that will surprise and confront its readers. Like Paterson at his best, Greenlaw has written new poems that are capable of entering 'the life of memory and everyday circulation.'

# Michael S Begnal

Mary O'Donnell, *September Elegies*, Lapwing, 2003, no price given.
Tony Curtis, *What Darkness Covers*, Arc Publications, 2003, £8.95.
Rosita Boland, *Dissecting the Heart*, Gallery Press, 2003, €17.50/€10.00.
John F Deane, *Manhandling the Deity*, Carcanet, 2003, £8.05.

Mary O'Donnell's *September Elegies* is published by Lapwing Publications, the Belfast press known primarily as a publisher of chapbooks. This is more or less a full collection, however, and perfect bound. The first thing one notices about the volume is its bare-bones production values. I have to say this put me off somewhat, though it seems almost uncharitable to mention. I realise that poetry publishers aren't exactly awash in cash. Nonetheless, Lapwing ought to have been able to come up with a more effective design and layout, even on a tight budget. There are some relatively affordable print-on-demand printers out there who would have done a better job. O'Donnell's work deserves it. Not to say that *September Elegies* is a perfect collection – there were some aspects I didn't like about it – but there were also certain key things that eventually won me over.

O'Donnell is able to articulate a world-view in her poetry without necessarily resorting to facile statement. She sets things down in a partic-ular way – that is, through particular images and language – and draws from them implications about the human condition. And the conclusions that she arrives at are usually quite uncomfortable in their verity. Much of the collection is about death (as befits its title). While the likes of 'Dawn Rain', 'Doctors, Daughters' and 'Pietà' are straightforward elegies for a father dying of a terminal illness, 'Field Work' is an example of what seems to be O'Donnell's forte: a rather obvious metaphor sustained until the poem is somehow believable. Because there is an immediate reaction here when we notice the metaphor – the feeling that we've registered an artificial device. Yet O'Donnell forges ahead, and with such prowess that we end up embracing it despite ourselves. In this poem, life is 'symbolised' by the work of the field. All the while there is 'the approaching, relentless thresher, / blades spinning at sunset, / the rustle of tumbling husks, / kernels borne away by encroaching dark': i.e., ageing, death. It's so obvious, but read those lines, those particular words, and you nod slowly in agreement.

In 'The Other Half' and 'A Marriage', O'Donnell sets up dichotomies. In the former, the artificiality of an aquarium versus 'the fray of real tides'; in the latter, the known world versus the unknown. These poems inhabit liminal spaces – usually a shore, or, in 'A Marriage', an Aran Island cliff:

> We are at the front line. Here
> things dance and tilt with light and dark,
> with halo and hoof, with what is sealed
> and what is cloven.

Often, though, O'Donnell dwells on the mundane, the dullness of day-to-day existence, just as she looks to define herself and her poetry in opposition to this. Many of the poems seek transcendence or a sort of elusive purity, as in 'Summerhouse Dream' where the real houses of rents and mortgages are contrasted with a dream-house in which the 'suburban silence' is supplanted by 'bedding down / before uncurtained windows'. 'My Irish Picasso' is a portrait of a would-be painter, the husband who has abandoned an artistic vocation for 'his daily bread, / the half-drunk coffee, dregs and sediments.' It is as if O'Donnell fears the same for herself. For the reader, the plenitude of humdrum detail she allows into her poems can sometimes be a drag. Again, though, there is a dichotomy. The other side to it all is O'Donnell's own art, the poetic bursts that produce work like 'The Library of Silences' (which could be the collection's masterpiece) and validate life even in the shadow of death. Here, at the conclusion to *September Elegies*, all of O'Donnell's themes and techniques are united and concentrated to stunning effect.

Arc Publications, the English publisher of Tony Curtis's *What Darkness Covers*, could teach Lapwing something about production values. They've obviously used an on-demand digital printer, but it looks great. The work itself, however, is somewhat more problematic. Curtis can occasionally be arresting, as in 'Small Interior' (which is written as a series of postcards), or 'Gallery: Twelve Poems after Paintings by Lucian Freud', or in the balmy 'Lemon Tree':

> It is so hot here now
> I have spent all afternoon
> in its sandy shade
>
> imagining you here,
> dressed only in an open kimono,
> the wind revealing you
>
> to me at her will
> as I sip sweet tea,
> the little moons of lemon,

like this
abandoned love,
bitter to the end.

More frequently, he treats the theme of lost love as an opportunity to moan about his own life. In most instances he employs a listless confessional voice, not unlike that of Paul Durcan. Part four of 'Asylum' (subtitled 'I Miss You') ends with the banal revelation, 'I now know / what you mean about dust. I miss you, / but first I need to set everything straight.' Curtis seems tired, unsure of himself. On several occasions, similarly to O'Donnell perhaps, he questions his own vocation as a poet. 'Nude' depicts his relationship with the muse in stark terms: 'There were nights / I could have died for her. / Now there's an awful / pattern to our lives.' 'Snowlines' ends with the revealing stanza, 'As for poetry: / this is another plan / that has gone all wrong.' But where O'Donnell is still able to plumb the depths of her creative soul and come up with something spectacular, Curtis plummets into inanity. For example, 'Trowel (after Allen Ginsberg)':

I have seen the best minds of my generation destroyed by DIY.

Get it? Then there's 'The Olympians', in which history's great poets are depicted competing in a footrace. It's a predictable gimmick, but it allows Curtis the opportunity to crack a few more jokes. Look, there's Shakespeare in lane three, 'his run will depend / on impeccable rhythm'; unfortunately the Romantics have all tested positive 'for opiates'; still, it's nice to see Dylan Thomas 'finally up on his feet'; and on it goes like that – 'It is poetry in motion'.

   It's not as if Curtis in unaware of what's going on here. Maybe he thinks that by exposing his own poetic foibles they will be excused. The poem 'Critic' reads like an attempt to subvert the criticism he anticipates for this collection. In this mock review, ironic reference is made to the 'twaddle of love and loss', 'the mire of profane / vapid verbiage' and so on. The best thing about the poem's unnamed book is 'the triptych that is sublime' – the three blank pages at the end. Curtis is probably being a little too hard on himself, but all told I don't think he could disagree with the observation that something is a bit off here, poetically speaking. If he's really in such a dysfunctional relationship with his muse, as portrayed in several of these poems – the ending to 'Nude' has him on his knees 'begging her to stay' – then perhaps the couple might still seek some sort of relationship counselling.

   The youngest of the poets presently under consideration, Rosita Boland has yet to become afflicted with the late middle-age angst of Curtis and O'Donnell. In *Dissecting the Heart*, she instead wraps herself in the blissful ignorance of the short lyric. The poems in this slight volume are framed primarily as a series of vignettes, occasions that lead to some ostensible insight. Often they are informed by scientific knowledge or visits to museums. Boland is of course best known for her journalism with *The Irish Times*, and many of these could have been expanded into interesting newspaper articles. As poems, they tend toward the formulaic. 'Teeth' is as good an example of this as any. Most of the piece is taken up with a scattering of historical points – that nobles once paid fees 'for pulling teeth from the poor' ('the first false teeth'), that 'teeth were extracted from the fallen / of the American Civil War and shipped / to Europe for re-use by the wealthy', and that the Nazis took gold fillings from the mouths of concentration camp victims. Then Boland interjects some minor observation at the end, in this case that

> There must have been men and women
> who went on to wear those circles of tainted gold
> on their wedding days:
> the rings like open shining jaws
> waiting for a chance to bite.

Except possibly for those last two lines, she is merely conveying facts. In some pieces (such as 'May Day') the observations are so bare they seem more like notebook entries than poems.

In 'Gold', Boland describes the Gleninsheen Gorget and its discovery in a Burren crevice. Here the lesson has to be deliberately spelled out for the reader: 'To look at this gorget is to realize / that discoveries are always possible'. Other poems function as metaphors for relationships, and can be quite hackneyed: 'We got shipwrecked / on the rocks of each other…' ('Shipwreck'). Equally, in the title poem:

> The heart has become the definable tissue
> that stands for the indefinable:
> for what makes us quicken and enliven,
> for what pulses through us and between us.

This is stating the obvious, as Boland does throughout the volume. It must be comforting to many readers to have their clichés reaffirmed. For this very reason, however, and because some of the poems (like 'The Astronaut's Wife') are in fact quite polished, I suspect that *Dissecting the Heart* will have a certain mass appeal.

John F Deane is a Catholic religious poet; so neither is there any existential crisis in *Manhandling the Deity*. Instead there is faith. As in much of his previous work, Deane's primary concern is 'to test out ways of living in the contemporary world while navigating by the lights of traditional belief' (as the back cover blurb has it). In 'Between Clay and Cloud' he states his credo outright:

> I believe in God
> self-broken and incomplete,
> in the creating pulse of his self-regarding love
>
> that spun the universe and its derivatives;
> that he created man in his own image
> self-broken and incomplete.

This vision of a broken God, Christ on the cross, is central.

Writing through this prism, Deane's poetry is unsurprisingly imbued with Christian values, his world described by Christian terminology. Thus the singing of blackbirds is a 'psalmody' ('Between Clay and Cloud'), bluebell flowers are 'nuns-of-Mary / in a huddle' ('Out of the Ordinary'), the hawthorns are 'like Moses' bush in flames' ('On Firm Ground'), etc. Inversely, Deane also wants to humanise God to some degree, to see him (in Christ) broken as man, in sombre cityscapes, in the wrangles of worldly existence: 'Lord you have touched and known us; we / have only old scores to settle, old drums to beat' ('Psalm'). The meaning of the collection's title soon becomes apparent. Though Deane is on the firm ground of Catholic faith, he is not blind to the harsh realities of life. A homeless person sleeping in a doorway is 'the very image of God's abdication' ('In a Shop Window'), while in 'Runt Bird' the speaker observes that 'the universe that claims us / thrusts on, beautiful and without compassion.' Nonetheless, there's still the sense that there's another world waiting, 'that everything beyond the rule and filthying of men / is whole, and holy, and unsoiled' ('House Martins').

Without verging wholesale into the arena of theology and philosophy, certain obvious problems arise if you don't share Deane's religious faith. Viewing *Manhandling the Deity* strictly as a poetry collection, I must say I found the constant asseveration of the author's ideology somewhat tedious. Consequently my favourites were those anomalous pieces where God wasn't necessarily so omnipresent, such as 'Frenzy' ('old man astounded again / at the frenzy that is in all living') or 'For the Record'. The latter vaunts the heroic intensity of a cat 'grown / perfect in wilderness', who, run over by a car, summons the strength to climb over a wall in order to die alone:

> Silent and intent it sucked pain
> into failing lungs, shivering, till a low, scared

wail of agony began. A time, and again
silence.

Where Catholic art is traditionally sensuous and exuberant in its execution,
Deane appears (to me) somewhat dour. As probably the most famous
Catholic poet, Hopkins should be an obvious antecedent here; but what
Hopkinsonian joy may be present in Deane's work is far out-weighed by
the overarchingly bleak portrait he paints of human existence. Technically
he is very accomplished – of this there is no doubt – but his method is
workmanlike rather than primal: 'I believe / in verses, the worked-for
inspiration, / the enabling image and fortuitous conjunction...' ('Between
Clay and Cloud'). Though the collection is expertly crafted, it would have
been somehow more satisfying to partake of that old, unmediated pagan
ecstasy (if, like Robert Graves, you believe that poetry has its roots in
ancient religious ritual), as opposed to the hierarchical, structured
institution that is Deane's Church.

# Michael Cronin

'BUT WHAT LANGUAGES DID THEY SPEAK?'

Charles Tomlinson, *Metamorphoses: Poetry and Translation*, Carcanet, 2003, £11.66.
Michael Hartnett, *Translations*, edited by Peter Fallon, Gallery Press, 2003, €20/€13.90.

In the late 1980s a large international gathering of translators in the Dutch city of Maastricht had as its motto, 'Translators Mean Well'. Good intentions in translation, however, are rarely enough. This is not simply because intention and execution are warring arts. The recurrent difficulty for translators in national literatures is that their intentions, successfully realised or otherwise, are largely ignored. How many English Departments in these islands offer courses on poetry in translation beginning, say, with Golding's 1567 translation of Ovid's *Metamorphoses* and ending with Carson's translation of the *Inferno*? Why despite the inspired intervention of translators in the literary history of English do anthologies regularly marginalise the contribution of translation, so that we get a hopelessly distorted picture of earlier periods such as the English eighteenth century or the Irish Literary Renaissance?

As a translator, anthologiser and critic Charles Tomlinson has laboured over the years to restore translation to its rightful place in the English literary canon. In *Metamorphoses: Poetry and Translation*, Tomlinson gathers together a collection of prefaces, reviews and a set of lectures that all bear on the topic of translation. He sees those who write about poetry as too often hostage to the Romantic fetish of the original with its suspicion of anything that might be considered secondary or derivative. Seeing translation as the idle by-product of the Promethean imagination in standby mode leads to a failure to appreciate the dual function of translation in literate societies, 'in all the great examples of how to do it [translation], the matter is two way – the poet-translator is extending his own voice, is sometimes writing his finest work, and performing a trans-mission of civilisation in the process of extending his own voice'. Tomlinson's heroes are Augustan. He contends that if Dryden had completed his *Iliad*, the course of English literature would have been radically altered. He defends Pope against those critics who would see his Homer as hopelessly domesticated by the monotonous economy of the couplet and shows how Pope was ingenious as well as bold in his transla-tion solutions. Tomlinson makes a case for Dr Samuel Garth's 1717 compilation of translations of Ovid's *Metamorphoses* as one of the finest collections of texts the language possesses. Garth's work is virtually unknown outside the more obscure corners of the academy and the failure to focus on the transformative energies of translations means that the Chaucerian strains in the work of Christopher Marlowe and John Dryden go largely unnoticed.

For Tomlinson, translators of poetry need not necessarily be poets all of the time but they must be poets once they engage in the act of translation. Here he quotes Charles Sisson and his 'ineluctable law', namely that '"a verse translation has to be done in the only verse that the translator, at the time of writing, can make; and that if he could not make verse before he will not suddenly become so gifted because he is faced with a classical text."' Tomlinson's gripe is with the dead hand of scholarship and a dogged exactness that lowers living texts into the grave of erudition. Contrary to the tiresome mantra of poetry being what gets lost in translation, Tomlinson agrees with the 17th century translator John Denham that translation is all about addition not loss, that in '"pouring out of one language into another, it will all evaporate' if 'a new spirit be not added in the transfusion."' Tomlinson is frequently attentive to the materiality of poetry in translation, what is added and how, and his discussion of the English-language translations of Horace, for example, is reasonably technical in places but the detail is a way of signalling achievement on the part of the translator rather than an idle display of pedantry on the part of the critic. Occasionally, a certain donnishness can haunt the sentences and there is an inescapable port-stained plumminess in the affection for titles ('Mrs. Feinstein', 'Dr. Webb') and the plaintive swipes at our 'Latinless present'. The set of lectures on the idea of poetry and metamorphosis previously published by Cambridge University Press in 1983 make much of the obvious connection between translation and the notion of metamorphosis and in particular of Ovid as the chief ancestor of literary modernism in the twentieth century. Tomlinson has very suggestive readings of what metamorphosis might entail. In a re-reading of Eliot's musings on tradition and the individual talent the English poet suggests that one of the functions of translations in Eliot's work is to open up the self to past instances of what it is like to be something else, something different. As a result, 'What the individual talent loses is the unnerving, unnerved sense of naked homelessness and lonely complaint. What is found is that human woes, though specific to oneself in the uniqueness of one's situation, are no longer homeless or condemned to formless outcry.' Metamorphosis, then, and translation by extension, is as much a matter of homecoming as departure or even exile. The treatment of Pound's translation activities is particularly interesting in this section of the book and Tomlinson has much to say about the two extraordinary years in London between 1913 and 1915 where Chinese poetry and vorticism will help Pound to concentrate on line as the unit of poetic expression and move away from fluent slackness of the Edwardian narrative. *Metamorphoses: Poetry and Translation* has the inevitable repetitions of the *post hoc* collection of separately published pieces, but the book is admirable in its informed and generous homage to the centrality of translation in the successive revolutions of the Word in English.

The new volume of Michael Hartnett's translations edited by Peter Fallon is an important contribution to a fuller understanding of Hartnett as poet. The writer that emerges from this collection is a poet who is clearly situated in and influenced by the tradition of Poundian modernism with occasional nods in the direction of Lowellian imitation. The original languages of translation include Chinese, German, Old, Middle and Modern Irish, Latin, Latvian and Spanish. Hartnett freely admits in the case of his Lao-tzu and Sikong Tu translations that he knows no Chinese but in this, of course, he was not markedly different from Pound who was heavily dependent on Ernest Fenollosa's scholarly cribs. By displaying the breadth of Hartnett's linguistic interests, *Translations* complicates the image of Hartnett as a *sui generis* native scholar-poet uniquely preoccupied with the internal linguistic traditions and tensions of this island. Indeed, in the careful attention to the strong poetic line and the sharp contrasts of lyrical juxtaposition, Hartnett's translation practice is clearly in keeping with the preferred modes of expression of poet-translators associated with the Translation Workshop tradition in the United States in the 1960s and 1970s.

The choice of Catullus and Horace too as Latin poets to translate is hardly accidental not only because, as Tomlinson demonstrates in the case of Horace, in particular, these two poets have had a long line of linguistic suitors in the English-speaking world, but because they are also the preferred poets of those poets, British and American, inspired by Lowellian liberties. The superlative achievements of Hartnett as a translator from Irish are already widely acknowledged, so the real revelation of this collection is his set of translations of the *Gypsy Ballads* by Federico García Lorca. Hartnett's uncanny instinct for correct word choice, appropriate repetition, and balance without predictability are fully explored in his lively and dramatic recreation of the Spanish originals. He avoids the lexical showiness and narrative tricks that can often mar translators working in the US Translation Workshop tradition. *Translations* raises larger questions about what we do to poets when we use the border protocols of cultural nationalism as the only way of understanding what poets do. Hartnett's public engagement with the language question in Irish writing has led to a tendency to frame his work in terms of the conflicting polarities of Irish and English, as if writing for Hartnett was a kind of fraught zero-sum game. But when Hartnett's *Translations* is read in the context of Tomlinson's *Metamorphoses* the perspectives shift. Whether it is the poetic career of the 17th century English poet Abraham Cowley or the shifting interests of an Irish poet such as Hartnett working in the late twentieth century, it is often more instructive to see translation not as a secondary activity but as a primary context. In other words, it is the metamorphic in-betweenness of translation which allows a poet like Hartnett not so much a breathing space as a way of going forward, a means of holding several different identities, languages and traditions together in creative co-existence. When Hartnett translates two lines of the Tao Te Ching as follows, 'Yes, they have left fine temples – / but what language did they speak?' his own answer is in *Translations*. They spoke many languages (translation) and one (poetry).

Tony Frazer

ARTICULATE AS A DANDELION

Christopher Middleton, *Of the Mortal Fire: Poems 1999-2002*, Sheep
Meadow Press, Riverdale-on-Hudson, NY, 2003, $12.95.

Middleton is a magician and the magic has not dimmed with the passing
years. Few poets writing in English today possess his ability to construct
such highly-wrought word-things, their music dense, the words an
intoxicating rush of 'rightness' but nonetheless fitted together with a rare
craft, nary a join to be discerned. Assonance, alliteration, end-rhyme,
half-rhyme and more besides; the full armoury is on display, and glitter it
does.

And why are these words here? Well, it's the very stuff of poetry;
they're here to enchant, to enlighten, to mesmerise, to leave the reader
with that flash of realisation that it *was* just so, yes, and a gasp, a shock
that visions can be communicated thus. Miracle indeed, in these parched
days of limited song, less thought, and minimal craft.

Derided often enough in English environs for being an aesthete (a
word that, to English ears, conjures images of absinthe, a curl of
cigarette smoke, a dozen identical grey suits, frock-coated perhaps, and
an impenetrable air of superiority), Middleton is in fact one of our
premier *observers*. But he is a particularly well-read, well-travelled, and
polyglot observer, and a voluntary expatriate these past 35 years and
more. Not that you'd realise the latter from the well-modulated tones of
his voice: no impression there from all those years in Texas. The American
south-west has cropped up in his poems in the past, but these days
France, Germany and, above all, Turkey seem the paramount locales for
his observations, studies – or perhaps *études*, for music rides these words
almost imperceptibly from page to ear, to inner ear. And the music has a
subtle rhythm, a cadence, a structure that is all too rare these days; is that
perhaps why he is criticised here? Because the reviewers have no taste,
their palates so dulled by years of over-boiled, monochrome gruel that
they can't deal with the flights of fancy and erudition on display in a
book like *Of the Mortal Fire*, or its fine predecessors?

And what does observation mean in the context of these poems?
Well, it means that someone with an eye has caught a detail. He's no
mynah bird, mindlessly transposing what's there into random cackle;
there's no mimesis here, for what's the point of a meditation on, say, a
Rembrandt painting, which got it so right in paint that most observers'
words just stumble around looking embarrassed? A painted canvas, an

awning in Cappadocia, a coffee in Paris or Istanbul, all trigger thoughts,
trains of thought that, converted into poetry, serve to enchant rather
than document.

Articulate as a dandelion,
Up through a crack, here
Between slabs, tombs, paving stones,
What a world sprang up to defend itself,
And has become, this too,
An uttermost of worlds, a breather;

Or else Caracci, catching his breath,
Simply had to tell the duo and the boatmen
Why he made rectangular, to catch the oval
Undulant eye's attention, this rift in time
Their beauty issues in and out of –

Content anon to dwell
On earth as refuge, while, as may be,
Other planets rising will subside.

— from 'Caracci: A River Landscape, 1600'

Middleton's late style has settled into a mixture of the elliptical lyric and
the meta-narrative. The ostensible subject-matter of the poems is often
foreign lands, art, history and exotic cultures, but they are more often
than not merely jumping-off points from which the author sets off, musing,
into the world of language – a compressed environment where all spare
words have been excised and the remainder operate in virtuoso mode.
There's not a lot of redundancy in these poems. Take the opening poem,
the beautiful 'Memory of the Vaucluse':

In this French September light
Picking out profuse

Corals that invade the vine,
Yellows in the hayrick

And pools of blue somehow
Round the rooster's comb,

To die – undiseased,
Tending a lavender field,

A naked eye
Braving the angel who descends

As angels on the loose
Holycards in a junkshop do,

Still with time enough –
Fear forgone, bondage to speech

Waved away – to sense the feathers
Rush and whisk,

Then giving up on it
To stand, the more to live.

This poem typifies his elliptical method, and his understated style. I'm
fortunate enough to have been in the Vaucluse several times and the
colours and natural elements here are very much drawn from nature, but
the key to the poem is that it is not a descriptive vacation-type piece (the
bane of all amateur poetry readings), but a working through of memory.
Memory is never reliable, and it has a habit of putting some things in
bold relief, while losing others of equal import, and fleeting impressions
can take on the appearance of reality, as those holycards in the junkshop
fuse with the angel who descends. No, I don't know who or what the
angel is but, frankly, it doesn't matter. The apparently clear surface hides
a number of pitfalls, deceptions, and syntactic manoeuvres that confound.
But it's beautiful, and it's true, and little else matters.

*Of the Mortal Fire* is one of the best books of verse to come my way in
2003. It's a wonderful experience to realise that someone's still out there,
capable of writing like this. If only others would realise.

The above text also appears in the print version of *Shearsman* 57 and is reprinted
with permission from Tony Frazer. Text copyright © Tony Frazer, 2003.
Shearsman Books website is at http://www.shearsman.com/

## Pickings and Choosings

DENNIS O'DRISCOLL SELECTS RECENT PRONOUNCEMENTS ON POETS AND POETRY

'Anyone who begins a sentence "as a poet I" is probably not a poet. It's like calling yourself a saint.'
– Michael Longley, *Colby Quarterly*, September 2003

'Poetry makes some kind of claim of honesty. If, at a party, I say I'm a poet, people have a hard time responding, almost as if I'd said I'm a priest.'
– Tobias Hill, *The Independent*, 9 August 2003

'Poets have always been young men in a hurry, desperately seeking to establish a poetic reputation before being prematurely swept away by death in the form of bizarre boating accidents, duels, battlefield mishaps, bottles of arsenic or one of the traditional picturesque illnesses such as consumption or syphilis.'
– Suzi Feay, *Independent on Sunday*, 24 August 2003

'Poems, one realizes, depend so much on whatever contemporary notion of the "poetic" was fashionable at the time that reading them years later one cannot escape being struck by how much they sound alike.'
– Charles Simic, *New York Review of Books*, 3 July 2003

'A poem is like the person at the table who won't speak unless everyone else hushes to listen. A poem is like the person whose tone announces *Enough of your jabber. Now I shall speak words worth remembering. You should want to chisel these words in marble.*'
– Mark Halliday, *The Georgia Review*, Summer 2003

'I have never been a great reader, which is probably why poetry appeals to me; you don't have to ruin your eyesight studying it, only carry it around with you and smell it from time to time.'
– Hugo Williams, *Poetry News*, Summer 2003

'Contemporary poetry is missing both the voice of public responsibility and the ear of the responsible public – a kind of high, morally serious agreement between poets and their readers.'
– J Bottum, *The Weekly Standard*, 4 August 2003

'It's hard to maintain there was ever a public role for an American poet. Whitman and Dickinson were essentially unknown to their contemporaries, although Whitman claimed to be speaking for all of us. No one knew.'
– Charles Simic, *Newsday*, 25 October 2003

'Our poetry covers a narrower path than it should and, consequently, it occupies a smaller niche in American culture than it should. Its specialized nature is the result of pruning away most everything that is unsightly and unruly, including the comedic.'
– William Waltz, *The Blade*, August 2003

'A society and a country stand to gain so much from having the most inclusive poem they can.'
– Eavan Boland, *RTE Radio 1*, 18 August 2003

'Our tendency to judge poets and poems by what side of a controversy they take, or by their efficacy in moving an audience towards one or another side, makes the most depressing feature of the discussion of poetry now, especially inside the academy.'
– Stephen Burt, *Contemporary Poetry Review*, August 2003

'I consider the division often made between politics and poetry to be thin and contrived…Separating them is a luxury. Literature is about life.'
– Jack Mapanje, *The Scotsman*, 5 August 2003

'"What does this line mean?" is the most intelligent question you can ask of a poem.'
– Craig Raine, quoted in *The Guardian*, 23 August 2003

'A common (and sloppy) view of Confessional Poetry is that it exposes the writer's self *in toto*. In reality, it merely shows us a different part of the self, and not necessarily the part that is most interesting.'
– Robert B Shaw, *Poetry*, October 2003

'The lyric poem…is the social act of a solitary maker. It situates feeling in language and seeks to restore human connection.'
– Edward Hirsch, *The Georgia Review*, Summer 2003

'Poetry does not court relevance, except to life's permanent conditions.'
– Sean O'Brien, *The Sunday Times*, 10 August 2003

'If a poem does not come from life but only from an idea, its effect is terminated with the working out of that idea.'
– David Constantine, *Poetry London*, Autumn 2003

'Nothing overtly significant need be happening in a poem. The doors of perception may be no bigger than a speck of dust, but when any one of them opens it is as if the whole of life were swirling behind it.'
– George Szirtes, *The Irish Times*, 16 August 2003

'My poems almost always start in some kind of memory…It's like a little beeper going off in your mind. Some little thing wakens excitement, and it gets connected with some other things. Ideally, it's like an avalanche – a little pebble begins to move, gathers a lot of energy and multiplies itself.'
– Seamus Heaney, *The New Mexican*, 26 September 2003

'Poetry wants to be contagious, to be a contagion. Its syntax wants to pass something on to an other in the way that you can, for example, pass laughter on. It's different from being persuasive and making an argument. That's why great poems have so few arguments in them.'
– Jorie Graham, *The Paris Review*, Spring 2003

'[Robert] Lowell's decline begins shortly after *Near the Ocean*, whose opening poem also contains the dated and sexist couplet "All life's grandeur / is something with a girl in summer".'
– Tom Paulin, *The Observer*, 3 August 2003

'[Robert Lowell] knew a lot about both grandeur and girls, but only he would have thought to link the two words in a line of verse, capturing thereby not only the *tendresse* of a sunlit affair, but also the way in which even the most frivolous, the most laughable, loves can make life seem a noble venture.'
– John Banville, *The Irish Times*, 9 August 2003

'The best love poems are known / as such to the lovers alone.'
– Les Murray, *The New Yorker*, 19 May 2003

'There…continues to be a kind of suspicion that poetry is high-minded and we can't understand it. But, at the same time, there is this kind of first-love relationship to poetry, which comes from nursery rhymes, from things that we loved in school when we were in love with learning.'
– Deborah Garrison, *The New Yorker Online*, 8 September 2003

'Today there is a danger in forgetting the pleasures of a poetry that is truly reflective, that involves more than the momentary and the instant, that evolves and is dynamic in its evolution.'
– N S Thompson, *PN Review*, July/August 2003

'Poetry complicates us, it doesn't "soothe"; it helps us to our paradoxical natures, it doesn't simplify us.'
– Jorie Graham, *The Paris Review*, Spring 2003

'If you write whatever it is well enough – Wallace Stevens is a good author to demonstrate this with – the reader will put up with quite a lot of incomprehension…'
– Robert Pinsky, quoted in *Contemporary Poetry Review*, October 2003

'The best poets are communicators – they need to make themselves heard…Modernists and theorists are always seeking to lure this ancient art form away from its roots and strengths towards some intellectually fortified bunker on the outskirts of obscurity.'
– Simon Armitage, *The Independent*, 24 October 2003

'With many poetry editors paying more heed to peer approval than reader response, and poetry's sly spin doctors trying to foist their academically distorted version of contemporary poetry on baffled readers, it's not surprising that bookshops see poetry as a minority interest.'
– Neil Astley, *Poems of the Year*, 2003

'We could say that great poetry is about something more important than poetry; we could even say that that's what makes it poetry.'
– Bruce F Murphy, *Poetry*, August 2003

'Some of our finest poets are unreliable judges of their own work, publishing too much of what they write (perhaps some publish more than they write).'
– Steven Cramer, *Poetry*, July 2003

'Most poets write and publish far too much. They forget the agricultural good sense of the fallow period. The Muse despises whingers who bellyache about "writer's block" and related ailments.'
– Michael Longley, *Colby Quarterly*, September 2003

'A poet who publishes many books of poems – seven, nine, eleven books – seems to say *I am special in fresh ways, cornucopically, every year, every month. Deeply revealing apprehensions of the great truths of life come to me so often – much more often than they came to Hopkins or Eliot – that I astound myself.*'
– Mark Halliday, *The Georgia Review*, Summer 2003

'The fact that [Robert Lowell] was a compulsive reviser does not make him a successful perfectionist, any more than one would say that a compulsive hand washer had a model hygienic regime.'
– James Fenton, *New York Review of Books*, 14 August 2003

'One should try and curb the need to make a poem too perfect. Maybe one should just try and get some spontaneity in; get it down and forget about it. That's really what's going to live of the poem. So finishing it off is just vanity.'
– Hugo Williams, *BBC Radio 4*, September 2003

'When the energies implicit in the activity are exhausted, when there's really nothing more to say, nothing that won't be just trying to pad out a little more, you know a poem's done.'
– Robert Creeley, *Rattle*, Summer 2003

'Free verse is ruthless in exposing when it lacks poetry. Any flabbiness in the line shows up very quickly…'
– Andrew Hudgins, *Image*, Spring 2003

'It is often said to be free verse poets who are in danger of wittering on with nothing much to say, because it's so easy. But poets who are extremely skilled and practised in rhyme and metre…may be in a similar danger of knocking off sonnets simply because they can.'
– Sheenagh Pugh, *Poetry Wales*, Spring 2003

'The thing that poets need to do is avoid writing "Poetry" with a capital P and in quotation marks.'
– Billy Collins, *Washington Post*, 29 August 2003

'I call the impulse to write poetry "the enemy", because it's trying to keep you poor. All the time and energy you pour into writing a poem is time and energy you won't be using writing something that's going to pay for the groceries.'
– Clive James, *RTE Radio 1*, October 2003

'No one could ever accuse him of daring to submit his talent to commercial interest. In fact, there were times when he looked like a tramp, and I suppose he didn't eat much more than a tramp.'
– Leon Atkin, on Dylan Thomas, *The Guardian*, 8 November 2003

'I don't think that it is essential to encourage the whole world to write. If you need to write, you will write. I don't think you can ask someone to teach you how to do it. They can't anymore than they can teach you how to live.'
– Olena Kalytiak Davis, *Anchorage Daily News*, 29 September 2003

'It's good to be discouraged. I've responded better to discouragement than to pats on the back. Because they're challenges.'
– Billy Collins, *Poetry London*, Autumn 2003

'Poets go crazy when somebody else wins an award.'
– Gerald Stern, *Rattle*, Summer 2003

'Poets today are running writing courses, editing, reviewing, judging poetry competitions, working in arts administration. All that may pay the rent, but it doesn't please the muse.'
– Suzi Feay, *Independent on Sunday*, 24 August 2003

'To write poetry you don't have to like it.'
– John Kinsella, *Agenda*, Summer 2003

'Poetry in America has declined to a civil war, a banal derby between two awful teams, and in Britain to a variety show (a royal variety show)…It's as though the human reef of literature was not considering any more applications, or the escalator had ground to a halt.'
– Michael Hofmann, *London Review of Books*, 11 September 2003

'Depending on who you read, Sylvia Plath was variously perfectly normal, oppressed, manic, depressive, manic-depressive, schizophrenic, a borderline personality, a psychopath, a sociopath, a nymphomaniac, addicted to sleeping tablets, the victim of an Electra complex, a masochist, and very definitely a misogynist. Or was that a feminist?'
– John Brownlow, *The Guardian*, 22 August 2003

'If we conflate current hostilities in critical and biographical accounts… T S Eliot emerges as a closet-homosexual, misogynistic, Jew-baiting, reactionary snob.'
– Stephen Romer, *Times Literary Supplement*, 14 November 2003

'At a time when Woolf is a racist and Larkin a womaniser, it is frankly amazing that Byron of all people continues to elude politically correct reassessment, especially given that his vices exceed those of any other writer I can think of, with the possible exception of the Marquis de Sade.'
– Duncan Wu, *The Independent*, 10 September 2003

'Among the things I remember him telling me was that he…had ten children by ten different women. It was his ambition as a poet and artist to make enough money to entertain all ten mothers, together with their children, at a jamboree which would take place in a tented oasis somewhere in the Sahara.'
– Meic Stephens, on Ted Joans, *Poetry Wales*, Spring 2003

'Alexander Pushkin drank like a frat boy, treated and spoke of women as whores, alternately rebelled against and toadied to the tsar, reduced his family to penury by addictive gambling, and typically allowed his usually dirty fingernails to grow long and claw-like… He could be utterly thoughtless of others' feelings but was himself "morbidly sensitive to. . . appearing comic" and quickly roused to anger, jealousy and spite.'
– Michael Dirda, *Washington Post*, 16 November 2003

'Without our poets, we really don't have a heart.'
– Walter Mosley, *National Book Awards Ceremony*, 19 November 2003

'It is almost eerie, the number of people who want to be poets.'
– Louise Glück, *New York Times*, 29 August 2003

## The Cat Flap

'It's a dull time for poetry. When did you last read something that electrified you? It's a time of women's poetry, lesbian poetry, gay poetry, black poetry, poetry translated from Moldavian dialects, gypsy poetry, handicapped poetry, computer generated poetry, minorities and majorities poetry, poetry against the war, poetry for the peace, poetry against plastic bags, poetry for creative cyclists.'

So begins 'Dylan Lives!' by John Hartley Williams in the current issue of *Poetry Wales*, one of a number of pieces that consider Dylan Thomas fifty years after his death in November, 1953. Hartley Williams argues that we need the 'fizzling work' of Thomas now more than ever – 'Thomas's great poems crackle and fizz like a sub-station gone mad' – and compares him to Charlie Parker. Both 'performed at white heat, or did nothing.' The issue also features a substantial piece by Dublin-based Nerys Williams, on a poet of an altogether cooler energy, Michael Palmer, and an essay by Margot Farrington on James Laughlin's groundbreaking press, New Directions. The continued liveliness and commitment to international poetry of that press is illustrated by Lyndon Davies' review in the same issue of Israeli poet Aharon Shabtai's polemical collection *J'Accuse,* and Russian poet Gennady Aygi's *Child-and-Rose*. *Poetry Wales*, edited by Robert Minhinnick. Submissions: Robert Minhinnick, Poetry Wales, 11 Park Avenue, Porthcawl CF36 3EP Wales. Subscriptions: Poetry Wales, 38-40 Nolton Street, Bridgend CF313BN.

*

> Morning star shines
> and I'm still out with the girls/lads
> God what a disgrace
> making my way home in the early morning.
>
> Morning, here it comes.
> I'm going home
> and I'm taking my loves with me
> we'll all walk home together.
> I'm going home late
> I'm going home at ten. Way!

The above is from 'Seven Transylvanian Songs' by Peter Riley, a suite of songs based on sung texts in Hungarian and Romanian. It appears in the *Electronic Poetry Review*, an online journal dedicated to publishing poetry, as well as interviews with poets, essays, and book reviews. The editors,

Katherine Swiggart and D A Powell, solicit most of the poetry that is published in *EPR*. 'However we do welcome submissions of essays, book reviews, and translations. All questions or suggestions should be sent to the editors.' It's an impressively ambitious magazine. Each of the six issues produced so far has offered an impressive range of work. The most recent features work by thirteen British poets, an interview with Christoper Reid, and translations. The site – at **www.poetry.org** – is well designed and easy to navigate and read. Which brings me to this quarter's Cat Flap question # 1: what has the Internet meant for poetry publishing? The economics of print publication have always meant that the odds were stacked against small magazines, and though the techno-logical advances of desktop publishing and digital printing have made the physical production of magazines to a good standard more achievable (as well as adding to the labours of the editor, who, these days, is likely also to be found moonlighting as designer, typesetter, advertising manager and typist) they can't do much to persuade a reluctant bookseller to go so far as to stock the thing. How many interesting poetry magazines have you seen in Waterstone's lately? Remember that interesting Cardiff / Edinburgh poetry journal you were thumbing in Hodges Figgis last week? No, didn't think so. For cyber-fiends, though, the Internet has opened up new spaces unhampered by the logistics and please-send-your-invoice-to-Solihull foosterings of the print mag. There is something very pleasing about being able to send oneself to say, *Jacket*, John Tranter's long-standing and consistently interesting online poetry journal founded 'in a rash moment in 1997, to showcase lively contemporary poetry and prose'. One of the advantages of a web magazine is that it doesn't have to stick to the periodicity of print: each issue of *Jacket* is put together piecemeal so you can drop in and see it develop, along with future issues, and past issues are all there within easy reach. And it's all free. Most of the material is original, but some is excerpted from or co-produced with hard-to-get books and magazines, the idea being to help them find new readers. *Jacket* doesn't accept unsolicited poems but if you want to submit a review, article or interview, you can send a half-page synopsis with your return email address.

*Jacket* also exploits the non-linearity of the web; there are no page numbers here, and you read by inclination and association, following from poem to feature to critical piece several issues back: a kind of reading particularly suited to poetry. There are twenty two issues on the site; the current issue includes a substantial section in memory of Ric Caddel edited by Peter Quartermain. **www.jacketmagazine.com**

★

Founded in 1998 by Garrick Davis, the *Contemporary Poetry Review* 'is an online journal devoted exclusively to the criticism of poetry.' It describes its mandate as an attempt 'to provide the general reader with a guide to contemporary poetry, and to serve as an organ of intelligent criticism'. It wishes to encourage 'criticism that is clear, spacious, and free of academic jargon and politics.' Unusually for a poetry site, it is not free but works by subscription: $6 per month, or $18 per year buys you unlimited access to the archives. Among the features in the archives for last December and November are Garrick Davis on the Golden Age of Poetry Criticism; Marc Pietrzykowski on books by Ciaran Carson and Medbh McGuckian; James Rother with Part Two of his Anthology Wars; David Wheatley on Philip Larkin's 'Aubade'; J K Halligan on Tom Paulin; Ernest Hilbert on the career of Gjertrud Schnackenberg and DH Tracy looks at the life and letters of Randall Jarrell. You can read the current issue, a Robert Lowell special, free of charge. The *Review* also has a letters section which at the moment features a diverting row between the editor and G Tod Slone, editor of *The American Dissident*, of which the following gives a flavour:

> Dear Garrick: How utterly grotesque and sleazy of you to belittle my criticism, labeling it "Publish or Perish," as if my efforts to push the obsequious functionaries of the Academic / Literary Industrial Complex, including the likes of you, to read "rude-truth" commentary were and are made so that I might climb the dubious ladder of academe. I'm unemployed, for chrissakes! Whether I publish or not is wholly insignificant to my career at this point. How utterly shameful of you to keep your readers from consulting the other side of this argument by not placing my website URL with the letters you published. Christ, you should encourage them! What is wrong with you, Garrick? However did you end up the way you are? You behave like an infant! God help the Nation if it keeps on producing the likes of you...

The *Contemporary Poetry Review* does not publish poetry, so 'please do not submit your poetry to this review for publication' but it does accept unsolicited review copies. For further questions, or submissions: Contemporary Poetry Review, P.O. Box 977, Pacific Grove, CA 93950, USA. **www.cprw.com**     Email editor@cprw.com

*

*Poetry Daily* is a US based anthology which each day publishes online a new poem from books, magazines and journals currently in print. Poems are chosen from the work of a wide variety of poets published in the English language. 'The daily poem is selected for its topical or seasonal interest, as well as for its literary quality' and included with each poem are information about the poet and attribution of the poem's source. Part of the purpose of the site is to make it easier for people to find poets and poetry they like and to help publishers bring news of their books, magazines and journals to more people. 'Over 1,000 books of poetry are published in the United States alone each year, but they can be difficult to find, even in areas brimming with bookstores. The numerous journals presenting new poetry and poets are even more elusive.' Sound familiar to anyone? If The Cat Flap may be allowed a moment of purring vanity, it can report that *PIR* 77 was given a very nice feature indeed. The site has proved so popular that it has crossed the dark divide to print, and has just published a selection from its first five years online, *Poetry Daily: 366 Poems from the World's Most Popular Poetry Website* (Sourcebooks; ISBN: 1-4022-0151-6; December 2003; $14.95), edited by Diane Boller, Don Selby, and Chryss Yost, with advisory editors Rita Dove and Dana Gioia. **www.poems.com**

*

There are thousands of poetry-related sites out there in cyberia and this featurelet is only intended to nudge reader towards their own explorations of a medium that can be greatly liberating in the access it provides to interesting poets and projects. Many publishers have adopted the web as a secondary presence, though of Irish poetry publishers, only Salmon and Wild Honey Press have risen to the challenge. Carcanet, Arc, Bloodaxe and many others have excellent sites, though The Cat Flap's current favourite is the Shearsman site. Shearsman started off as an A4 photocopied magazine, and still home-produces an A5 version, but all of the magazines are now also on the web, and the magazine, site and publisher offer very interesting work. Irish readers may be familiar with Trevor Joyce's *With the First Dream of Fire They Hunt the Cold: A Body of Work 1966/2000*, which was jointly produced by Shearsman Books and New Writers' Press. Based in Exeter, England, Shearsman is a publisher 'of contemporary poetry in mostly late-modernist styles', and active since 1981. Shearsman in all its guises is directed by Tony Frazer, whose review of Christoper Middleton in this issue of *PIR* features as a Book of the Month feature on the site. The site also includes an opinionated Recommended Books section. Then there is the Shearsman Gallery, which serves as the online equivalent of a chapbook series. The latest publication in the series is *An Introduction to the Work of Michael Ayres*, which features poems, artwork, essays and commentaries, and is timed to coincide with the publication of a major new volume of the author's work, *a.m.*, by Salt Publishing of Cambridge. Plans for future publications in this series include a selection of over a hundred Spanish poems, translated by Michael Smith. **www.shearsman.com**

*

Although all of the above sites take advantage of Internet technology, the web is used primarily as a presentation tool, a means of publishing poems and material about poets and poems. But there are also many sites devoted to the creation of poetry online, which use the net as a way of organising interactive writing projects. Trevor Joyce has just started a new experiment at collaborative composition by members of the British and Irish poets Listserv, 'very distantly related to renga', and if you'd like to have a look at it, it's at **http: soundeye.org/offsets**

*

This concludes our mini survey-let of poetry sites. Next time The Cat Flap will go poetry blogging. Here, to keep you excited, is a taster from the web log (blog) of a US based Irish poet:

> 12.4.03
>
> It's a bitterly cold day in Providence.
>
> 12.5.03
>
> First winter snow in Providence.
>
> 12.6.03
>
> Looks like about 8 inches of snow in Providence.
>
> 12.7.03
>
> A sunless cold day in Providence.
>
> 12.8.03
>
> It's a sunny bright day in Providence, snow melting.
>
> 12.9.03
>
> Bird notes and snow drop in intense beads into Providence thaw.
>
> 12.10.03
>
> A pleasant grey day in Providence, snow in dirty heaps and damp clumps.
>
> 12.11.03
>
> A rainy dark slushy day in Providence, and blowy. Redolent and swampy.
>
> 12.12.03
>
> A sunny mild day in Providence.
>
> 12.13.03
>
> A sunny cold day in Providence.

# Notes on Contributors

**Louis Armand** is an artist and writer who has lived in Prague since 1994, where he currently lectures on cultural theory and art history at Charles University, and works as a freelance art consultant. His most recent books are *Strange Attractors* (Cambridge, 2003); *Momo Provoz* (Cambridge, 2003) and a volume of experimental prose, *The Garden* (Cambridge, 2001).

**Michael S Begnal** is a poet and critic, and editor of *The Burning Bush*. His collection *The Lakes of Coma* (Six Gallery Press) was published in 2003, while another, *Ancestor Worship*, is forthcoming from Salmon.

**Paddy Bushe** was born in Dublin in 1948 and now lives in Waterville, Co Kerry. He has published five collections of poetry, the latest of which are *In Ainneoin na gCloch* (Coiscéim, 2001), a collection in Irish, and *Hopkins On Skellig Michael* (Dedalus, 2001). He was awarded an Arts Council bursary to complete a bilingual collection, *The Nitpicking of Cranes*, based on journeys to the Far East, which will be published by Dedalus in 2004.

**Peter Carpenter** is co-director of Worple Press, and Visiting Fellow at the University of Warwick. A 'character' in Iain Sinclair's *London Orbital*, his most recent collection is *The Black-Out Book* (Arc, 2002).

**Austin Clarke**, the foremost poet of the generation after Yeats, was born in Dublin in 1896 and, between the publication of his first book in 1917 and his death in 1974, he published sixteen volumes of poetry, as well as novels, verse plays, autobiographies and essays. A *Selected Poems*, edited by Hugh Maxton, was published by Lilliput in 1991.

**Michael Cronin** is Director of the Centre for Translation and Textual Studies, Dublin City University. His most recent works are *Time Tracks: Scenes from the Irish Everyday* (New Island, 2003) and *Translation and Globalization* (Routledge, 2003).

**Tony Curtis**'s fifth and most recent collection is *What Darkness Covers* (Arc Publications, 2003). He is a member of Aosdána.

**Peter Didsbury** was born in 1946 in Fleetwood, Lancashire. He moved to Hull at the age of six, and read English and Hebrew at Oxford. He has published four collections with Bloodaxe: *The Butchers of Hull* (1982), *The Classical Farm* (1987), *That Old-Time Religion* (1994) and *Scenes from a Long Sleep: New and Collected Poems* (2003).

**Katherine Duffy**'s collection *The Erratic Behaviour of Tides* was published by Dedalus in 1998.

**Ian Duhig** was born in London in 1954 of Irish parents. He was educated at Leeds University, and now lives in Leeds. He worked with homeless people for 15 years in London, Yorkshire and Northern Ireland before becoming a freelance writer in 1994. His latest book, *The Lammas Hireling*, published by Picador in May 2003, was selected as the Poetry Book Society's Summer Choice and shortlisted for the T S Eliot Prize.

**Tony Frazer** is the editor of Shearsman Books.

**Eamon Grennan** teaches at Vassar College in Poughkeepsie and was 2002 Heimbold Professor of Irish Studies at Villanova University. His most recent books are *Still Life with Waterfall* (Gallery Press, 2001) and *Facing the Music: Irish Poetry in the 20th Century* (Creighton University Press, 1999).

**Ron Houchin**'s poetry has been nominated for the Paterson and Pushcart Prizes. His collection *Moveable Darkness* was published by Salmon in 2002.

**John McAuliffe**'s first book is *A Better Life* (Gallery Press, 2002); he is programming this year's *Poetry Now* festival in Dun Laoghaire, Co Dublin, and he lives in London.

**Sarah Maguire's** most recent collection is *The Florist's at Midnight* (Cape, 2001). She edited *Flora Poetica: The Chatto Book of Botanical Verse* (Chatto & Windus, 2001). The only living English-language poet with a book currently in print in Arabic, her selected poems, *Haleeb Muraq*, translated by the distinguished Iraqi poet, Saadi Yousef, was published in Damascus by Al-Mada House in 2003. Sarah lives in London where she teaches poetry translation at The School of Oriental and African Studies.

**Kate Newmann** is currently employed by Arts Care as Writer-in-Residence for the Down Lisburn Health Trust, by the Arts Council as Writer-in-the-Community in Ballycastle, County Antrim, and by Poetry Ireland in association with Sligo Education Centre. She has published *The Dictionary of Ulster Biography* and a collection of poetry, *The Blind Woman in the Blue House* (Summer Palace Press, 2001). She was the winner of the 2003 Listowel Poetry Competition (single poem category).

**Nuala Ní Dhomhnaill** was born in 1952 and grew up in the Irish-speaking area of West Kerry and in Tipperary. She has published a number of collections of poems in Irish, the most recent of which is *Cead Aighnis*

(Coiscéim), and a number of collections with English translations including *Rogha Dánta/Selected Poems* with translations by Michael Hartnett (Raven, 1986); *The Astrakhan Cloak* with translations by Paul Muldoon, (Gallery Press, 1992) and *Pharaoh's Daughter* (Gallery Press, 1990).

**Hugh O'Donnell** is a frequent contributor to *Poetry Ireland Review*. His work has appeared most recently in *Metre* and *THE SHOp*.

**Gregory O'Donoghue** is Writer in Association with the Munster Literature Centre. His collection *Making Tracks* was published by Dedalus in 2001.

**Dennis O'Driscoll's** recent publications include a selection of reviews and essays, *Troubled Thoughts, Majestic Dreams* (Gallery Press, 2001) and his sixth collection of poems, *Exemplary Damages* (Anvil, 2002). His *New and Selected Poems* will be published by Anvil later this year.

**Hans-Christian Oeser** was born in Wiesbaden, Germany, and now lives near Dublin. He has translated poetry collections by Judith Wright, Paul Muldoon and George Ellenbogen. With Evelyn Conlon he edited *Cutting the night in two: Short Stories by Irish Women Writers* (New Island, 2002). Forthcoming publications include an *ABC of Oscar Wilde*.

**Peter Porter,** born in Brisbane in 1929, has lived and worked in London since the 1950s. His first collection of poems *Once Bitten, Twice Bitten* appeared in 1961 from Scorpion Press. Among his many publications are *The Cost of Seriousness* (OUP, 1978); *Collected Poems* (OUP, 1983), which won the Duff Cooper Memorial Prize; *The Automatic Oracle* (OUP, 1987), which won the Whitbread Poetry Award; and most recently *Max is Missing* (Picador, 2001), for which he won the 2002 Forward Poetry Prize for Best Collection. He was awarded the Gold Medal for Australian Literature in 1990, and the Emeritus Award of the Australia Council in 1998.

**Gerard Smyth**'s most recent collection is *Daytime Sleeper* (Dedalus,2002).

**Richard Tillinghast** is the author of seven books of poetry, most recently *Six Mile Mountain* (Storyline Press, 2000). He has also published a critical memoir on Robert Lowell, and has a new book of criticism, *Poetry and What Is Real*, due out later this year.

**Macdara Woods** has published many volumes of poetry since his first collection in 1970. *Knowledge in the Blood: New and Selected Poems* was published by Dedalus in 2000. A founder-editor of the literary review *Cyphers*, he is also a member of Aosdána.

## Guidelines for Submissions to *Poetry Ireland Review*

### Poetry

– Send a maximum of six poems.
– Always keep a copy of each poem submitted.
– Poems should be original and previously unpublished, although previously published work may be included in *Poetry Ireland Review* at the discretion of the Editor.
– Poems should be typed, with the author's name on each sheet.
– If a poem continues over more than one page, continuation sheets should be clearly marked. If there is a stanza break between pages, this should also be indicated.
– A stamped self-addressed envelope should be enclosed to facilitate a reply. Submissions not accompanied by SAEs won't be returned.
– Overseas submissions should be accompanied by the appropriate number of International Reply Coupons.
– The Editor normally replies within 3 months.

### Articles and Reviews

– Reviews are normally commissioned by the Editor. *Poetry Ireland Review*, however, will consider articles or essays submitted, or proposals for articles or essays. Samples of previous work can also be included with an article, essay or proposal. Articles and essays should be double-spaced, with at least one-inch margins, and be between 1,500 and 3,500 words.

All submission and other communications to the Editor should be addressed to:

> Peter Sirr
> Poetry Ireland Review
> Poetry Ireland
> 120 St Stephen's Green
> Dublin 2

Email submissions of poetry are no longer accepted. However, if a writer includes an email address with his or her <u>postal</u> submission, we can forward notification of the editor's decision by email. In such cases the hardcopy of the work will not be returned.

# Poetry Ireland REVIEW
## IRIS ÉIGSE ÉIREANN

*"Vitally important for readers and writers,
always an excitement to open"*
SEAMUS HEANEY

## SUBSCRIPTION FORM

I would like to subscribe to *Poetry Ireland Review/Iris Éigse Éireann*

☐ from the most recent issue

☐ from issue number: _____

NAME _____

ADDRESS _____

_____

_____

_____

_____

TELEPHONE _____

EMAIL _____

*Please return to:*  Poetry Ireland,
120 St Stephen's Green
Dublin 2
Ireland
*Phone* 00353 (0)1 478 9974
*Fax* 00353 (0)1 478 0205
subscriptions@poetryireland.ie

## SUBSCRIPTION RATES

Full subscription
*Four issues of Poetry Ireland Review
plus six issues of Poetry Ireland Newsletter per year.*

| IRELAND/BRITAIN | OVERSEAS |
|---|---|
| ☐ One year: €30.50 | ☐ One year: €40.50 |
| ☐ Two years: €56 | ☐ Two years: €76 |

*Poetry Ireland News/Scéala Éigse Éireann only
(Free to subscribers to Poetry Ireland Review)Six newsletters per year.*

| IRELAND/BRITAIN | OVERSEAS |
|---|---|
| ☐ One year: €8 | ☐ One year: €10 |
| ☐ Two years: €15 | ☐ Two years: €18 |

Payment by Cheque, Postal Order or Visa/Mastercard
Cheques made payable to Poetry Ireland
I have ticked the appropriate box above and have enclosed € _____

CARD NUMBER: _____

EXPIRY DATE: _____

CARDHOLDER: _____

BILLING ADDRESS *(if different from above)*: _____

_____

_____

_____

# Previous Editors of *Poetry Ireland Review*

| | |
|---|---|
| John Jordan 1–8 | Spring 1981–Autumn 1983 |
| Thomas McCarthy 9–12 | Winter 1983–Winter 1984 |
| Conleth Ellis and Rita E. Kelly 13 | Spring 1985 |
| Terence Brown 14–17 | Autumn 1985–Autumn 1986 |
| Ciaran Cosgrove 18–19 | Spring 1987 |
| Dennis O'Driscoll 20–21 | Autumn 1987–Spring 1988 |
| John Ennis and Rory Brennan 22–23 | Summer 1988 |
| John Ennis 24–25 | Winter 1988–Spring 1989 |
| Micheal O'Siadhail 26–29 | Summer 1989–Summer 1990 |
| Máire Mhac an tSaoi 30–33 | Autumn 1990–Winter 1991 |
| Peter Denman 34–37 | Spring 1992–Winter 1992 |
| Pat Boran 38 | Summer 1993 |
| Seán Ó Cearnaigh 39 | Autumn 1993 |
| Pat Boran 40–42 | Winter 1993–Summer 1994 |
| Chris Agee 43–44 | Autumn/Winter 1994 |
| Moya Cannon 45–48 | Spring 1995–Winter 1995 |
| Liam Ó Muirthile 49 | Spring 1996 |
| Michael Longley 50 | Summer 1996 |
| Liam Ó Muirthile 51–52 | Autumn 1996–Spring 1997 |
| Frank Ormsby 53–56 | Summer 1997–Spring 1998 |
| Catherine Phil Mac Carthy 57–60 | Summer 1998–Spring 1999 |
| Mark Roper 61–64 | Summer 1999– pring 2000 |
| Biddy Jenkinson 65–68 | Summer 2000–Spring 2001 |
| Maurice Harmon 69–72 | Summer 2001–Spring 2002 |
| Michael Smith 73–75 | Summer 2002–Winter 2002/3 |
| Eva Bourke 76 | Spring/Summer 2003 |